The
Fundraising
Planner

The

Fundraising

Planner

A Working Model for Raising
the Dollars You Need

TERRY & DOUG SCHAFF

Jossey-Bass Publishers
San Francisco

The example concerning the Rhinebeck Chamber Music Society in Chapter Two is reprinted herein with kind permission of Carole Schaad.

The vignette entitled "Does It Have to Be Done This Year?" in Chapter Four, information about the World Monuments Fund in Chapter Six, and Exhibit 10.1 in Chapter Ten are reprinted herein with kind permission of the World Monuments Fund. These materials are copyright © World Monuments Fund, 1999.

The example concerning Amy Rosenfeld and The Working Playground in Chapter Six is reprinted herein with kind permission of Amy Rosenfeld Poux.

The "Sample Endorsement Letter" displayed herein as Exhibit 6.1 in Chapter Six is reprinted with kind permission of Terry Born.

Jossey-Bass books and products are available through most bookstores. To contact Jossey-Bass directly, call (888) 378-2537, fax to (800) 605-2665, or visit our website at www.josseybass.com.

Substantial discounts on bulk quantities of Jossey-Bass books are available to corporations, professional associations, and other organizations. For details and discount information, contact the special sales department at Jossey-Bass.

This book is printed on paper containing a minimum of 10 percent postconsumer waste and manufactured in the United States of America.

Interior design by Bruce Lundquist.

Library of Congress Cataloging-in-Publication Data

Schaff, Terry, date.
  The fundraising planner: a working model for raising the dollars you need/Terry & Doug Schaff.—1st ed.
    p.   cm.—(Jossey-Bass nonprofit & public management series)
    Includes bibliographical references.
    ISBN 0-7879-4435-1 (alk. paper)
    1. Fund raising—Handbooks, manuals, etc.   I. Schaff, Douglas, date.   II. Title.   III. Series: Jossey-Bass nonprofit and public management series.
HV41.2.S33   1999
658.15'224 — dc21   99-19903
                                                                                     CIP

FIRST EDITION
PB Printing   10 9 8 7 6 5 4 3 2 1

Contents

List of Figures and Exhibits

List of To-Do Exercises

Preface

How This Book Can Help You

THE PURPOSE of *The Fundraising Planner* is to prepare you to successfully assemble an operational fundraising plan that will help your organization meet its specific funding needs. This book is designed as a workbook. Each chapter shows you how to master an essential skill for raising charitable dollars and includes one or more exercises. These exercises are building blocks for your plan. Once you have completed them you will have a detailed road map for raising money for your nonprofit organization. You will have identified a core group of fundraising constituents; written materials that enthusiastically convey your mission, accomplishments, and needs; and targeted financial goals for selected donors. Preparing and using this fundraising plan is going to take some work. It won't happen overnight. But your reward will be your ability to design, launch, and control a dynamic fundraising campaign.

Nonprofit organizations come into existence to serve society in ways that the private and public sectors cannot do alone. From collecting healthy leftover food for distribution to the hungry to presenting chamber music concerts for local school groups, nonprofit organizations identify societal needs and then configure themselves to address those needs. Nonprofits often cannot charge the populations they assist for the services they provide. Even when they do, the income typically does not cover their expenses. Therefore fundraising is essential to every nonprofit organization.

Unfortunately, many fundraising efforts fail because the organization pays insufficient attention to creating a plan and monitoring its progress. A sound fundraising plan is your map and itinerary for raising the money your organization needs. It identifies your donors and prospects and your strategies for researching, cultivating, and soliciting them. It is your calendar of events, mailings, and strategies to attract contributions. It also tracks your progress toward your funding goal. The fundraising plan we present in this book will give you an essential overview of how to achieve your fundraising needs for the year. Because it has a flexible structure, you will be able to adapt it as the needs of your institution change and as you obtain new information.

Audience

This book is intended to meet the needs of a variety of people involved in fundraising. Those new to fundraising will learn the context within which the various fundraising activities of the organization are selected. How does the organization arrive at its fundraising goal? Which donors should be approached, and how can their contributions best be solicited? By becoming familiar with both the details and overview of a fundraising plan, those with less experience can become more comfortable and effective in their roles.

More experienced professionals should find it beneficial to compare their current planning methods with the methods presented here. They will find new ideas for making their fundraising plans visual and for improving their command of scheduling and their ability to coordinate all the different parts of their plans and to track fundraising progress.

Board members and other constituents who want to know more about the genesis of funding events and appeals will benefit from learning the rationales behind a fundraising plan. They may also benefit from the discussion on reporting, coming to understand how monitoring a fundraising plan can help the organization achieve its goals.

Finally, committed volunteers, employees, and contributors can gain knowledge of the details underlying their organization's fundraising process and be able to better involve themselves in achieving its goals.

Overview of the Contents

Part One presents an introductory discussion of the many tangible benefits of having a fundraising plan (Chapter One) and a step-by-step overview of the fundraising model developed in this book, which you can use to plan any fundraising campaign (Chapter Two).

The remainder of the book is divided into four parts that correspond to the main stages of designing a fundraising campaign as developed in the model. In each chapter, step-by-step analysis is accompanied by planning exercises. Real-life examples reflect the fundraising issues nonprofits are experiencing throughout the country.

Novice fundraisers will probably want to read the chapters in order, as each step of the planning process depends on knowledge learned in previous steps. More experienced fundraising professionals may wish to focus on selected chapters, to gain a deeper understanding of topics of particular interest to them.

Part Two, "Understanding the Big Picture," provides the reader with the foundation needed to construct a fundraising plan. Chapter Three goes over the methods you can use to accurately forecast the amount you need to raise. It also illuminates the assumptions involved in forecasting. At first glance your funding need may seem insurmountable. Chapter Four shows you how to construct a realistic overview of your plan and break your funding need into manageable parts, a step that can eliminate a lot of confusion and anxiety.

Part Three, "Deciding Plan Inputs," focuses on the central three steps of fundraising planning. It will help you to order the process of finding the prospects most likely to give to your organization and then selecting the most effective means of soliciting their support. Step one is building the case. In order to attract contributions it is essential that you present your organization clearly and in a compelling manner. Chapter Five shows how to create a core communications piece, starting with your organization's case statement. Creating this document is an essential first step in finding the best donors for your cause. Later this same document will become the basis of your funding proposals. Supporting your case with evidence is so important to successful fundraising as to be obvious, but it can't be taken for granted. Chapter Six explains how to plan which case support materials to gather and how to present them to prospects to gain maximum credibility.

Step two is identifying key donors. Unless you have a schedule of research activities, individuals who have the ability and interest to become major donors can slip through the cracks in your fundraising efforts. Chapter Seven helps you discover who your donors are going to be. Chapter Eight shows you how to evaluate prospective donors in order to decide how much time and attention to give each one. Chapter Nine focuses on the key constituency of your board of directors and explains how to mobilize them to raise money for your nonprofit.

Step three is selecting effective fundraising activities. Which activities are most likely to generate the dollars you need? Chapter Ten presents the most effective ways to plan your cultivation and solicitation activities. Despite the effort it may take to identify your best institutional prospects, receiving a grant or finding a sponsor can make a significant difference to your worthy cause. Chapter Eleven gives you a quick reliable way to find the best institutional donors for your fundraising plan and includes a special section on obtaining corporate sponsorships.

The fundraising model we describe has a flexible design so you will alter it as your needs change and as new information surfaces. Part Four (Chapter Twelve), "Putting the Plan Together," guides you through assembling your plan and presents a variety of the forms it can take. You will use all the exercises you will have completed by this point to create a visual road map of how your organization is going to raise the money it needs.

The ability to monitor the pulse of ongoing fundraising activities is a major benefit of a fundraising plan. Part Five (Chapter Thirteen), "Monitoring the Plan," leads you through the preparation and use of status reports that compare your current results to those projected in your plan. Tracking gifts received from key constituencies and the status of fundraising activities allows you to respond to areas that are under- *or* overperforming and to make adjustments when necessary so your fundraising plan will continue to meet its goals.

Finally, the Internet now offers nonprofits some new tools for fundraising, and the Appendix describes a number of useful Web sites for your research needs and suggests how you can get started with your own Web page.

February 1999

Terry Schaff
Doug Schaff
Red Hook, New York

The Authors

TERRY SCHAFF is director of institutional advancement for the Poughkeepsie Day School in Poughkeepsie, New York. A professional fundraiser and consultant, she has served organizations ranging from Lincoln Center for the Performing Arts and Bard College to pregnancy prevention centers and grassroots organizations feeding the hungry, such as City Harvest.

DOUG SCHAFF, author of *How to Make Money Investing Abroad* (1995), is a successful fundraising writer who has written grant proposals and fundraising literature for projects ranging from local youth and violence prevention programs to an international orchestra's world tour. Doug received an M.B.A. degree (1977) from the University of Chicago.

To our parents
Shirley and Norman Roth
Mary and Phil Schaff Jr.

Part One

The Fundraising Planning Model

Chapter 1

Why You Need a Fundraising Plan

FOR BUSY FUNDRAISERS, the idea of creating a fundraising plan can seem beside the point and the act of planning a waste of time: "We need to be out raising money, not creating hypothetical giving scenarios!" If your fundraising program relies on a few major donors, then maybe you can manage without preparing a detailed plan, as long as you can keep those donors at the top of your priority list, stay in close contact with them, and regularly review ways to ensure their continued support. Even in this simplified situation, however, you face the risk of losing stalwart supporters through unforeseen changes in circumstances. In addition, even if you're not planning your ongoing fundraising, you probably should be planning for the *future* health of your nonprofit and increasing your base of support.

If your fundraising involves researching, cultivating, and using various techniques to solicit dozens, if not hundreds, of prospects from the public and private sectors (individuals, corporations, foundations, and government sources), then the process can soon become difficult to manage effectively without a plan. The results of insufficient planning quickly become apparent: prospects are forgotten; mailings, cultivation events, and one-on-one solicitations don't get the attention they need; and the talents of the fundraising team are not maximized, which in turn means that the board members, staff, and committed donors upon whom the nonprofit relies fail to receive the attention they need.

There are many tangible benefits to planning. To begin with, having a plan allows you to carry out these three important steps:

1. *Focus on what is important:* understanding the big picture—the organization's funding need and how you plan to achieve it—allows you to spend your time wisely.

2. *Take care of the details:* deciding on the inputs to your plan—the tasks needed to achieve your goal—and ranking them improves your productivity.

3. *Track progress toward your goal:* preparing monthly progress reports that monitor the results of your fundraising plan gives you critical feedback—should a change in plan become necessary, you can make it.

Focus on What Is Important

Fundraisers are like jugglers; they always have several balls up in the air. While you're getting one mailing out, you've already got to start planning the next. You're in the middle of one event, and another starts tomorrow. Staying in touch with people who just gave is essential, but you've got to keep going out and getting other people to give, widening your net.

Juggling all these tasks—just keeping track of them all—let alone monitoring their progress, can be a tremendous challenge. We've all had the experience of missing the anniversary of a major donor's gift, finding out that a foundation application is due right now, or scrambling to get out one more special appeal for funding. It's not fun!

Fundraisers tend to be very creative, entrepreneurial people for whom the routine of planning is not immediately appealing. Many tend to rely on their memories rather than reports and calendars. However, even if you have an excellent memory, you'll find that keeping yourself organized and on track will make it easier for you to identify and successfully complete all the fundraising tasks your organization needs from you.

Take Care of the Details

Creating a schedule and sticking to it will improve your productivity. Conversely, missed opportunities can be sore reminders that planning improves fundraising results. Have you ever experienced grant application deadlines that somehow got away? Have you ever shared the galling experience of the development associate who heard that a donor to his organization had made a large gift to a similar nonprofit—just as the associate finished a quarterly review in which he admitted to "not having had time" to get around to that donor?

Once a social services agency that was relatively inexperienced in raising money from the private sector found a contributor who became a fairy godmother (the agency had previously depended on government grants and vouchers). This woman not only supported the agency personally but she asked her friends to give. She hosted a cocktail party to introduce her friends to the organization and followed up on the event with a written appeal. That combination raised close to $100,000.

The following year, however, the nonprofit let all this momentum slide until nearly past the date when this donor group had previously given. In the midst of all the other demands on people's time, no follow-up event was planned and no solicitation letter drafted, even though the institution's fiscal year was drawing to a close. At the last minute, with the willingness of their fairy godmother, agency staff patched together an approach to salvage the situation and tried to recoup the gifts the agency had received the previous time.

In this case the agency recovered well under pressure. Personalized letters were drafted and signed just days before the fairy godmother went on summer holiday. The problem with any last-minute approach, however, is that it does not take maximum advantage of the opportunity available. In this case fundraisers had little time to analyze the previous gifts and the donors or to separate out the major prospects and prepare individual strategies for each of them. They could have solved this problem with a readily available visual overview of their fundraising plan. If they had *nailed it to the wall* and regularly referred to it, upcoming giving milestones for donors and contributions they were counting on would not have come as a surprise.

Fundraisers need visual checklists of tasks to complete. Most fundraisers need to keep in contact with many different funding sources, for example, so a schedule of donor and prospect contacts is very useful. Completing the exercises in this book will help you create an overview plan that will be available to your whole development team. This picture of your fundraising operation will help ensure that all your fundraising activities will get attention when they need it and not be forgotten. In Chapter Twelve, we go over how to make your fundraising plan visual, because when you can *see* the plan, it is easier to prioritize what needs doing and when.

With an overview plan in place, you can create lists of the major ways you get funds for your organization and add them to the plan framework. Specific fundraising activities and donor groups can become headings for mini-plans, with steps specified to achieve particular objectives. Without these mini-plans it's easy to lose track of important details about how you are going to raise the money you need and from whom.

Track Progress Toward Your Goal

The planning and scheduling techniques we go over in this book are tools to keep you organized, but as great a benefit is the flexibility you gain. By checking the progress of your fundraising plan you get critical feedback. (And if the plan is an icon on your computer screen or prominently placed on your wall, you can easily spot-check it.) Monitoring your plan keeps you in touch with reality. You can see areas that are lagging and zero in on them. You can produce regular status reports for key fundraising participants such as board members and staff. A plan by its very presence permits analysis of comparisons. As a result you are flexible; you can quickly respond to changing conditions, go after new prospects, alter appeals, or make any other necessary mid-campaign adjustments smoothly.

What Happens When There Is No Planning?

One of the problems with not planning is that you can lose confidence. Without a plan, obstacles may not be identified until they are fully developed and temporary dead ends can seem like the real thing. You can even fall prey to the myth that "there's no money out there for us." For over twenty years a friend of ours has been running a terrific big brother–type sports program for inner-city kids. When he doesn't have enough money from membership fees to meet his budget, he borrows and begs contributions and in-kind gifts from local stores and friends. He explained to us that a number of years ago he attended a meeting sponsored by a large foundation for nonprofits and prospective donors to share interests and concerns. He came away feeling disenfranchised and with the impression that "there is no money for us here. We don't fit in."

Receiving rejection letters in response to your appeal for support can have a similar effect. They can make you feel that there isn't any money out there, or at least not for your organization. The hidden assumption in that feeling is that the methods you tried covered every opportunity. However, the process by which generous contributions reach worthy causes is not that simple. Fundraising is somewhat like finding an apartment in a city without classified ads or real estate brokers. You might walk up and down twenty blocks and not find any vacancies, but that wouldn't mean there weren't any available. You might not be trying the right route. You have to try as many as you need to, until you get that apartment. Similarly, a failure to expand your funding base may simply mean that the methods you've tried haven't worked. That doesn't mean there aren't other methods that will.

Though our friend managed to operate his program successfully for over twenty years, it wasn't until he developed an annual fundraising plan that he learned how to communicate effectively with people who weren't already familiar with his program in order to gain their support. After he went through the same steps described in this book, his sports program received its first grant, increased scholarships, and added an academic assistance component. Now this vital, active community group is ready and eager to tackle other prospective funders. It's amazing how a taste of fundraising success builds confidence.

Eight Specific Ways Planning Boosts Fundraising Results

There are at least eight specific ways that planning can improve your fundraising results:

1. Planning prepares the organization for the long haul. Fundraising is a long-term process that requires continual effort. It doesn't happen overnight. Planning recognizes that. Don't begin a cultivation effort to recruit or solicit donors if you aren't in it for the long haul. Once you have started this process, don't drop it midway. A gift from a contributor represents a beginning. When you have got a donor's support, it is as important to schedule cultivation activities with that donor as it is to approach another prospective donor for an initial contribution. Your best prospect for a gift is someone who has already made a donation to your organization, your *worthy cause.* So don't ignore your active donors!

2. Planning helps you thoroughly research prospective donors. Schedule the time to put together a profile on each major prospect. To find the information, check the research tools listed in Chapter Eight and learn to use the on-line services described in the Appendix. Look at prospects from the standpoint of their personal lifestyles and activities and their business activities. Circulate their names on a confidential list to your development committee. Find out if someone affiliated with your organization has a personal or business connection or is able to add prospect information to what you have gathered.

3. Planning can make individuals a top priority in your fundraising. Almost 90 percent of philanthropic contributions are made by individuals. Foundations and corporations may look attractive. They have the contributions budgets, but individuals give away far more. As your top prospects, they deserve to be the subject of specific plans. Putting individuals first does not take away from the importance of foundation and corporate support, but remember to keep the facts straight: foundations and corporations contribute 9 percent and 6 percent of total giving, respectively ("Giving USA 1998," p. 22).

4. Planning takes into account the people already in your camp. Who supports you? Give those people your attention. If you put on concerts, for example, check your subscriber list, your ticket buyers, and others who benefit from your activities. Because they know you, these people are your prime prospects. Solicit your organization's lawyer, accountant, and everyone else it does business with, including the local restaurant your audience and staff frequent. And don't forget your volunteers. Ninety percent of

individuals who volunteer for a nonprofit also contribute financially to it (Hodgkinson and Weitzman, 1994, p. 30).

5. Planning encourages you to use every contact you have. In fundraising, nothing takes the place of personal contact. Being asked to give by someone you know and respect has a powerful effect; in fact, in our opinion, it is the most significant factor that leads to higher giving levels. So before soliciting a prospective major donor, plan to find someone who supports your worthy cause and who also has a personal relationship with the prospect. Ask your organization's board members, staff, and lawyer. Ask friends and clergy. In short, ask anyone connected to your worthy cause. Ask your contact to introduce you to the donor and, if possible, to make the gift request with you.

6. Planning helps you put your best foot forward. People like to support a winner. Appeals that say, in effect, "We're in dire straits; we can't meet our operating budget," will make people question the effectiveness and efficiency of your organization. Put your best foot forward by giving people positive reasons for supporting your project. What are the hopes and dreams of your worthy cause? Prepare a communications piece that shares these hopes and dreams with your donors; then let donors know why you are uniquely qualified to realize these goals.

7. Planning can turn rejection into opportunity. Being turned down can lead to a productive talk between you and your prospect about the prospect's interests. If you are prepared and can remain positive during discussions with prospects about their concerns and their initial decision not to fund your project, you may discover areas of common interest and begin building a relationship. And that relationship can eventually lead to a major gift.

8. Planning ensures that everyone gets treated as a prospective donor. People who have benefited directly from your worthy cause are not your only prospects. Anyone who shares a sense of urgency about your group's mission is a likely donor. Keep a lookout for these prospects!

Chapter 2

How the Model Works

STRIPPED TO ITS ESSENTIALS, fundraising planning is not complicated. It is nothing more than naming the fundraising tasks the nonprofit needs done, figuring out who will do them, and establishing a timeframe for doing them. Scientists, however, have confirmed that people's brains can focus on a maximum of five to seven pieces of information at once. (Even that seems high!) Fundraising requires a person to focus on many more pieces of information than that, so a fundraising plan helps the fundraiser get around this limitation. It acts like a map, with specific directions to guide your development efforts so that you can accomplish the goals necessary to keep your nonprofit going. Rather than weighing down the fundraising effort, a good plan will enable you to communicate more effectively and coordinate your organization's activities better. That way you will actually spend *more* time fundraising and *less* time managing the whole process.

As we outlined in Chapter One, once planning seeps into an organization's thinking, it can have big benefits. The Rhinebeck Chamber Music Society, for example, annually presents eight chamber music concerts to a local audience. The board used to occupy itself each month with scrambling to figure out how to remind people about the next concert and convince them to become subscribers. Now, instead of sending one subscription mailing and then creating a new little note every month, the board organizes all these materials before the concert season begins. This one-time organizing and scheduling has freed the board to spend time doing other kinds of creative fundraising. For example, it has gotten local restaurants to sponsor the postconcert receptions. Planning the concert promotions freed the board to consider a membership mailing separate from the subscriber mailings. Increased emphasis on planned fundraising has also led the Rhinebeck Chamber Music Society to add preconcert talks. The preconcert talks are not an automatic fundraiser, but hopefully, by doing them, the society will build an audience, and therefore a larger base of supporters.

A Model for Any Fundraising Campaign

Every nonprofit requires its own fundraising plan, based on its activities, purposes, and donor base. Some nonprofits emphasize mailings to solicit donors, others concentrate on one-on-one cultivations, and still others focus on membership drives. Don't worry; you don't have to change your fundraising style to take advantage of the techniques presented in this book. We have developed a general fundraising planning process that everyone can use.

This fundraising model is shown in Figure 2.1. It contains four basic sections: understanding the big picture, deciding plan inputs, putting the plan together, and monitoring the plan. Each section contains topics that mirror the question-and-answer process that all fundraisers go through when developing a fundraising campaign. We have used this model as the pattern for organizing this book, so you can find a discussion of any part of the model by turning to the similarly titled section of this book.

The fundraising plan is the place to record, refer to, and add your answers to questions such as these:

- How much money do we need to raise?
- Where is it going to come from?
- Whom will we approach and how?
- What research do we need to do?
- When is the right time to ask for a donation?
- Once we get a gift, how do we follow up?
- How soon after we get a gift can we ask again?

The rest of this chapter introduces each of the planning topics, which are then more fully described in the later chapters.

Understanding the Big Picture

The first thing you will do is look at your organization's financial statements (its income and expenses) to determine what funds you have to raise. You are going to break your institution's funding need into manageable parts by analyzing where last year's funding came from, who

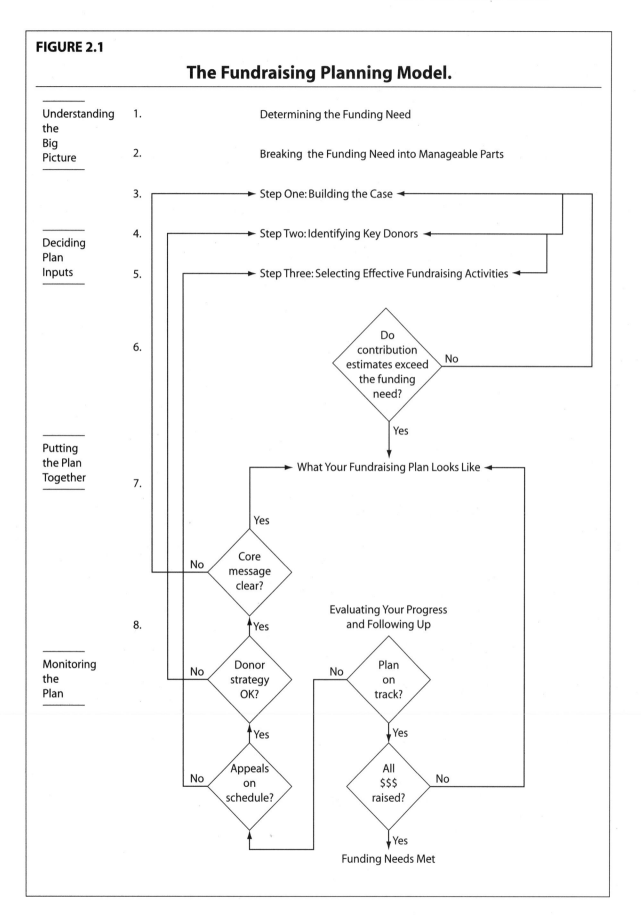

FIGURE 2.1

The Fundraising Planning Model.

Understanding the Big Picture

1. Determining the Funding Need

2. Breaking the Funding Need into Manageable Parts

Deciding Plan Inputs

3. Step One: Building the Case

4. Step Two: Identifying Key Donors

5. Step Three: Selecting Effective Fundraising Activities

6. Do contribution estimates exceed the funding need? — No / Yes

Putting the Plan Together

7. What Your Fundraising Plan Looks Like

Yes — Core message clear? — No

8. Evaluating Your Progress and Following Up

Donor strategy OK? — No   Plan on track? — No

Yes

Appeals on schedule? — No   All $$$ raised? — No

Yes

Funding Needs Met

Monitoring the Plan

your largest contributors were, and what changes are expected in those patterns.

Once you have a clear sense of how much money needs to be raised, how much is expected in repeat gifts, and how much must be raised in new and increased contributions, then you can begin strategizing about where and how you are going to secure these funds. Looking at how your organization is perceived by donors, you will create a list of potential new contributors with matching interests.

Determining the Funding Need

Get the facts! Go to the bookkeeper. Review your organization's past and projected budgets, its operating income and expenses. Ask such questions as these: What have been the giving trends? What percentage of contributions has been in restricted funds? What percentage has been unrestricted? How much has come from earned income? How much has come from contributions? How much are the different categories of income expected to increase (decrease) next year? What multiyear pledges are on the books? What percentage of last year's gifts is projected to be renewed? How much is needed in contributions? How much *new* money (increased gifts and new contributions) needs to be raised?

Breaking the Funding Need into Manageable Parts

Ask yourself, How have we raised money in the past? From what categories of donors have we received it? Look at who has given what. Once you have answered these questions by reviewing historical gift records, then you will ask, How did we attract those gifts? What fundraising activities has this nonprofit engaged in to cultivate and solicit gifts? This is what breaking your funding need into manageable parts is all about.

Next you will create an outline of all the different things you do during the year, all the top categories of fundraising techniques you have used. Do you solicit money from individuals? If you do, make that a category of your fundraising plan. Do you solicit money from foundations? If so, use that as another category. Do you get government funding? Put that as a category. Do you seek funding from institutions or associations? Put that as a category. Do you run events? Do you have membership? Do you conduct certain special events?

Based on this work, you will list amounts that you reasonably estimate (or even guesstimate) will be raised from each donor category and fundraising activity.

Deciding Plan Inputs

This is the heart of your fundraising plan, where you will determine all the activities large and small that lead up to your securing contributions: submitting grant applications; responding to the anniversaries of major gifts; designing and conducting fall, winter, spring, and summer mailings; holding special events; conducting productive board meetings; and so forth. From the deadlines and dates associated with these activities, you will produce detailed work schedules of what needs to be done each week to complete all your fundraising activities successfully. Later you will arrange this information on your planning calendar. The more accurate the activities list the better, but don't be worried that your first planning effort has to be 100 percent accurate. This is your first draft, based on the best information you have at the moment. As you research and gain more information, your activity list will change and grow more detailed and complete.

Step One: Building the Case

As you design your plan, you will create a core communications piece and select the materials to support the importance of your organization's work.

Creating a Core Communications Piece. Donors receive thousands of funding requests each year. In order to get their serious consideration, you have to present your organization in a clear and compelling manner. An organization's *case statement* is the basic message it wants to communicate to constituents; it tells people why the organization exists. You will use your organization's case statement to plan a standard proposal that answers these questions: What is the organization trying to accomplish? What makes the organization special? How much money does the organization or program need to raise? How will the organization evaluate its programs? What has the organization achieved? Who supports the organization now?

The answers to these questions will form the basis for a standard proposal that can be adapted to create communications ranging from letter appeals and membership updates to phonathon scripts and benefit committee invitations to grant applications.

Selecting Case Support Materials. How does your organization become known for the important work it does? If prospective donors have not heard of your group, how do you catch their attention and express that your nonprofit is worthy of support? Case support boils down to credibility, a belief by others that your organization will accomplish its goals and objectives. Donors expect you to show *evidence* that you are good at what you do.

You need to plan which case support materials to gather and how to present them in a cohesive, attractive package. From letters of endorsement to donor lists and recent news articles, what you have in your case support kit will depend on the message you are trying to get across to your donors. Some items clearly need to be included, such as a brief biography of the leader of your organization and a list of your board of directors. In this stage of your fundraising planning, you will also pull together communications pieces to develop a standard set of public relations documents for your worthy cause.

Step Two: Identifying Key Donors

Your plan should help you recognize, track, and evaluate donors. In addition, it should guide you to make the best use possible of the fundraising potential of your board of directors.

Recognizing Potential Donors. Now it's time to get specific about identifying the best prospects for your nonprofit's worthy cause. Which prospects have the highest chance of meaningfully contributing to it? Which could substantially increase their gift amounts? The best prospects are current supporters, people already involved with your organization. Therefore it's important to organize the process of finding them.

Who participates in your organization's functions? Who donates time or money to your cause? Who has had a previous relationship with your charity? Who has been helped by your charity? Look for relationships that will lead you to people who are familiar with your organization, who care about it, and who may very well want to contribute to it. Creating a schedule of research activities to answer such questions will greatly assist the process of finding individuals who have the ability and interest to become major donors.

Tracking and Evaluating Prospective Donors. In order to easily reach people connected to your nonprofit (its *constituents*), you will have to plan how to keep track of these prospective donors. In the old days fundraisers maintained donor information on 3-by-5-inch notecards. In small and large nonprofits alike, certain data should be kept in hard-copy files. However, with computers generally available these days, many nonprofit organizations should consider using generic database products or specialized software designed to track donor information. These computerized records should contain such information as the prospective donor's name, address, and giving history, a status report, and a follow-up plan.

Once you have your constituent lists organized, you will ask which individuals or categories of prospective donors you should spend the most time cultivating. You don't have the luxury of spending a lot of time with every prospective donor, so you will need a method to evaluate them. Chapter Eight offers a ranking system that you can use in this part of your planning to determine what efforts to devote to each.

Involving Your Board. Every nonprofit organization needs fundraising support from a committed board of directors. Ideally, each board member cares enough about the nonprofit to support it financially; that means giving money. But there are other ways board members can help, such as making fundraising calls, hosting cultivation events, or otherwise drawing contributions to your group.

How do you mobilize the board of directors to raise money? No fundraising plan is complete without addressing this issue. Your board members have the potential to be fundraising leaders, yet all too often they have little idea of how to fulfill this role. They may feel uncomfortable with volunteering the names of friends and business acquaintances who could be prospective donors. They may not know how to approach a major donor for a contribution. They may not understand their responsibility to be contributors themselves. To increase their leadership effectiveness, you need to learn board members' strengths and interests and to encourage them to use their abilities, matching these abilities with the organization's needs.

Step Three: Selecting Effective Fundraising Activities
Fundraising activities focus on both cultivating and soliciting individuals and finding appropriate institutional donors.

Planning Your Cultivation and Solicitation Activities. After identifying your most likely individual prospects, you will begin to generate a list of cultivation and solicitation activities for your fundraising plan. Specific fundraising activities vary widely, from benefits and auctions to incentive giving and membership and subscription drives. Which ones are best suited for your nonprofit?

In general, the people already connected in some way to your nonprofit will respond best to your fundraising, whatever method you are using, and the stronger the connection the better the response. Conversely, those with little or no connection will be less responsive. Nevertheless, to get the best response, the fundraising activities you select should be appropriate for the specific donors you are trying to reach, even if they already know your organization. To help you find the best cultivation and solicitation techniques for your donor prospects, Chapter Ten explores the six principal ways most nonprofits cultivate donors and ask for money: face-to-face requests, fundraising events and benefits, personalized letters, telephone appeals, scheduled mailings to in-house lists, and direct-mail "Dear Friend" letters.

Finding Institutional Donors. Finding your best institutional prospects and filling out their grant applications can take considerable staff time and energy, but the pay-off can go beyond securing a potentially large gift. Receiving an institutional grant can increase public awareness of your organization and add credibility to your organization's cause, which is always helpful when soliciting new donors.

Chapter Eleven presents an approach to ranking institutional prospects that is similar to the one in Chapter Eight for ranking individual prospects. It is a quick, reliable way to identify the best institutional donors for your fundraising plan. These days there is so much information available on corporate and foundation giving that part of the key to success is to avoid getting bogged down in the library prospecting for institutional donors. Conducting an efficient search means *minimizing* the time you spend finding and soliciting corporations and foundations.

Putting the Plan Together

You can design your fundraising plan to show a wide variety of perspectives. Once you have gathered all your research materials and described your cultivation effort and schedule of solicitation activities, you will format all this information to see it the way you want to and at the level of detail that makes the most sense for your organization. Two key pieces to putting your fundraising plan together so it functions as a visual overview are *calendars* and *activity schedules.*

Your fundraising calendar will give you a visual timeframe for your mailings, benefits, and other fundraising activities. It will act as a flow-chart of activities for the whole year. When you lay out the key steps for getting your mailings out, putting on events, and making cultivations and solicitations, you will be able to see the times when you have too many activities scheduled and the gaps where little is planned.

You will construct your fundraising calendar on the basis of activity schedules for your organization's individual development projects. These lists of the steps, or tasks, needed to stage each activity you have planned are also a specific way to view your overall fundraising plan. There are many steps to putting on a benefit, for example, from forming a benefit committee to printing and sending invitations. Each step needs a timeframe and deadline. And each activity should have its own activity schedule listing all its tasks with their timeframes and deadlines.

You don't need a computer program to create your plan. However, there are computer programs available that do make it easy to expand or contract the level of plan detail you want to look at. For example, you can look at

- Summary overviews: see how much you expect to raise from each donor category and by when.
- Activity schedules: see details within each summary donor category and fundraising activity. For example, if you solicit foundations, you can call up a list of those you intend to submit proposals to and the requested amounts.
- Assignments: see who is responsible for each task and who else is assisting.
- Current activities: see your plan by calendar day, week, or month, according to what activities you want to focus on.

Monitoring the Plan

When you can track who's doing what and the due dates, you gain control over the fundraising process. If something does go wrong—a deadline is missed or a cultivation takes longer than expected—tracking reports allow you to quickly zero in on the problem's source and respond, minimizing the impact on your fundraising plan. This speed and flexibility increases your chances of raising the money your organization needs.

After the launch of your fundraising campaign, your plan becomes a valuable tool to help you direct and fine-tune the organization's efforts. A quick look at progress reports shows what's going right and what's going wrong. It's easy to see which tasks need prioritizing, which need more of your time now, and which ones are going to require some extra help.

As we suggested in the previous chapter about the benefits of having a fundraising plan, with progress reports, you can track development by comparing your original estimates to what's been done, identify problems before they cause a loss of income, and more easily make midstream changes that will help you reach your fundraising goals sooner.

Moreover, as you raise the money your nonprofit needs, it's important to make sure you are keeping donors informed about the organization and its activities. A fundraising plan can help you avoid leaving donors with the feeling that they hear from you only when you want a contribution. When you pay appropriate attention to donors, raising money from them should be easier the next time.

At this point, we suggest you start evaluating your current level of fundraising planning by completing To-Do Exercise 2.1. The exercises are an important part of this workbook with real-life applications. You can use the information you gather with these exercises as you create your own fundraising plan, and you can apply the questions they raise and the methods they illustrate to your daily fundraising activities. We have provided space for your answers to shorter questions. Please use separate sheets of paper for longer activities.

TO-DO EXERCISE 2.1

Applying the Fundraising Model to Your Organization

Using the fundraising model in Figure 2.1 as a checklist, review a development activity that your organization was recently engaged in. Answer these questions:

- What went right?

  _____
  _____
  _____

- Where could the activity have been improved?

  _____
  _____
  _____

- Did you determine what the funding goal was? How did it compare to what was raised?

  _____
  _____
  _____

- Did you break the overall goal into manageable objectives? What could you have done to improve this step?

  _____
  _____
  _____

- What prospects did you decide to concentrate on? What others would you have liked to include? What methods did you use to involve them in the event? How effective were these methods?

  _____
  _____
  _____

- How did you track the various parts of the plan for the activity?

  _____
  _____
  _____

Part Two

Understanding the Big Picture

Chapter 3

Determining the Funding Need

IT IS A WELL-KNOWN TRUISM that donors give money to effective charitable programs; they do not contribute simply to cover a nonprofit's financial needs. However, a fact of nonprofit life is that program and administrative expenses exceed revenues (for example, income from ticket sales, membership dues, or investments). How much money needs to be raised in philanthropic dollars this year? Each nonprofit organization needs to accurately forecast this amount so it can set about raising that sum.

The fundraising plan evolves out of the organization's funding need. The amount of money the development office needs to raise can be summarized in a number, but there are some very human assumptions behind it. Before you begin estimating where contributions will come from, it is important for you to become familiar with the thinking behind your organization's funding need.

Many development professionals are handed a funding goal by the executive officer of their nonprofit or by its board of directors and asked to come up with a strategy for meeting it. Whether or not you have input into setting your nonprofit's funding goal, there are several benefits to knowing how the decision makers arrived at this number.

Financial statements will be included with funding proposals, and you want to be generally knowledgeable about what is in them. They provide important background information about the dollar amount that needs to be raised. A comparison of this year's goal with previous years' goals will highlight some telling aspects of the numbers in funding requests. It can also prepare you to answer donors' questions. Understanding the background to your organization's funding need can even help you come up with prospect ideas and fundraising strategy.

Financial statements are put together according to generally accepted accounting principles (GAAP). But you do not have to have taken an accounting course or be an expert in bookkeeping to understand them. The question from a fundraising planning standpoint is, What is the best way to understand the numbers behind the funding request? This chapter seeks to answer that question in a straightforward, nontechnical way so that even if you have had a lifelong aversion to accounting statements, you will still be able to understand the thinking behind them.

Accounting's Growing Importance

For charities, bottom-line numbers have traditionally been of less concern than the services they provide. These days, however, to effectively solicit money from donors, a nonprofit organization has to deliver an accounting that accurately portrays its finances and also conveys a sense of cost consciousness. Foundations and corporations have a fiduciary responsibility to make sure their gifts are given to legitimate charities with an ability to follow through on their stated intentions. Today it is more important than ever for a nonprofit's projections of income and expense to be grounded in reasonable assumptions.

An organization's *funding need* is the difference between its total operating expenses and its income other than private and public support. The same equation can be used to determine the funding need for specific programs. Here are some key definitions to help you understand this equation:

- Funding need: operating expenses minus total income other than private and public support

- Operating expenses: all sums spent on programs, salaries, fundraising, general administration, and operations, including supplies and purchases

- Total income: all income from private support, government grants or donated goods, and all other sources of revenue, such as investments, sale of capital assets, fees for services rendered, and sale of products (for example, T-shirts and cards)

- Private support: cash donations, in-kind gifts (for example, donated equipment and office supplies or valuable art works), and other gifts from individuals and companies

- Public support: grants from government sources

- Restricted income: contributions designated for a specific purpose

- Unrestricted income: contributions received for general operating purposes

Laying the Groundwork for Estimates

The executive director, director of finance, and board of directors take into account the organization's financial history in order to come up with the current year's funding need. They find this historical portrait of the expenditures and income in the organization's *financial statement* for any given year. Because the financial statement shows what actually happened previously, its data are important factors underlying current financial estimates. Expanding or contracting program needs and other factors can be estimated separately. But everything else being equal, it makes sense that the organization's recent financial history will, to a reasonable extent, repeat itself.

Your development office may have copies of the previous year's financial statement. If not, the director of finance or comptroller does. When you take a look at it, typically you will see that the difference between total income and total expenses is a small positive (credit balance) or negative (deficit balance) number. The National Charities Information Bureau (NCIB) standard is that a charity should "not have a persistent and/or increasing deficit in the unrestricted fund balance." Like a for-profit company with consistent losses, a charity that runs persistent deficits will go out of business!

The private and public support your charity received plus the negative balance or minus the positive balance is equal to last year's funding need. Several years' worth of financial statements will provide a fuller picture of the organization's typical funding need. Nonprofit managers take into account various historical ratios in operating income and expenses. They answer the following sorts of questions to more accurately predict what to expect in the upcoming year:

- What have been the giving trends?

- What percentage of contributions has been in restricted funds?

- What percentage has been unrestricted?

- How much has come from earned income?

- How much has come from contributions?

The Best Reason to Look at the Numbers

The best reason you should become familiar with fiscal numbers is that they can give you fundraising ideas and lead you to donors. Take a look at the income side of a financial statement. How many categories of income are listed? Each one represents a general source of income. Knowing that, you can brainstorm ideas to approach specific constituencies connected to these income sources and increase their contributions. This can work with whatever sorts of noncontribution income you have. One nonprofit we know has revenues from a concession stand. Looking at the income statement, a development officer came up with a successful idea to solicit and raise money from the concession stand vendors.

The Budget

Budgets are *predictions* of what will occur. They are projections, management's best guesses as to what expenses the nonprofit will need to incur in order to carry out its charitable purpose in the upcoming year and what funding it can expect. Budgeting can be creative but needs to be tied to realistic assumptions. The financial or bookkeeping department bases projected expenses on historical trends, known costs, and any new factors that the organization has identified. After answering the questions listed earlier about giving trends and historical sources of income, nonprofits then ask these predictive questions:

- How much are the different categories of income expected to increase (decrease) next year?

- What multiyear pledges are on the books?

- What percentage of last year's gifts is projected to be renewed?

- How much is needed in contributions?

- How much *new* money (increased gifts and new contributions) needs to be raised?

Existing nonprofits use financial statements to provide a logical basis for budgeted predictions. New nonprofits, who have no giving history or previous accounting statements, use budgets as their prime financial tools to back up funding requests.

Nonprofits need three types of budgets: an annual operating budget, an income budget, and a program, or project, expense budget.

The *operating budget* lists the total annual expenses of the nonprofit, including program, administrative, and fundraising costs. The Philanthropic Advisory Service (PAS) says that expenses should be reported in "categories corresponding to the descriptions of major programs and activities . . . (i.e., salaries, employee benefits, occupancy, postage, etc.)." They should include an "accurate presentation of all fund raising and administrative costs" (Council of Better Business Bureaus, Inc., 1982, p. 2). (For further information, contact an accountant willing to provide pro bono services; see the suggestions at the end of this chapter.)

The *income budget* tracks your institution's total income, broken down by various categories and by whether it is restricted or unrestricted. Typical categories are

- Membership dues
- Donations by source (for example, individuals, corporations, foundations, and government)
- Special events (net income)
- Gifts-in-kind
- Tuition
- Ticket sales
- Investment income
- Product sales

The *program, or project, expense budget* is essential to funding requests. (We use *program* and *project* interchangeably in this discussion.) A subset of the operating budget, the program budget lists all expenses associated with each particular program of your nonprofit. Whether the project is to restore your church's stained glass windows or to help out at a soup kitchen, the program budget is what you show donors to back up *what it's going to cost*. If your organization engages in one activity only, such as an after-school program for local grade school children, then it doesn't need a separate program budget; the operating budget is the program budget.

The expense categories the program budget uses should be selected as in the operating expense budget. The budget should pay particular attention to allocating administrative costs to each project. It should list each type of staff separately and estimate the percentage of their time that will be spent on the project.

The budget should list all actual and prospective sources of income for each project. Sources can be broken down into foundation, corporate, and significant individual supporters, with their contribution amounts for the organization's current and most recent fiscal year.

Advantages of Budgets

Budgets offer a number of specific benefits and opportunities to fundraisers:

• A budget puts your organization's funding request in concrete terms. This is essential for the donor. It allows donors to compare your project to others. It also shows whether the nonprofit is meeting certain standards of acceptability (in hourly rates paid to social workers or in amounts paid to artists-in-residence, for example).

• A budget clarifies your fundraising thinking. You clearly see what you need funding for. You need so much for salary, so much for supplies. Then, if you want to, you can package pieces of the operating budget or particular line items in order to request funding specifically for them. For instance, once you forecast your printing costs for the upcoming year, you can go to a donor or to a printer to get those costs underwritten.

• A budget helps you keep control of a project. It also helps you and the board identify problems before they occur, *and make the necessary adjustments.* This goes back to the way running a nonprofit is like running a business. To be businesslike it has to avoid spiraling costs. Without a budget the nonprofit won't be able to respond as quickly to spending more than it takes in. With a budget, if costs begin to get larger than forecast, you will be able to respond to the problem before it gets totally out of hand, by analyzing why it is happening and where the organization can cut back.

• A budget allows donors to hold the organization and its leadership and staff accountable. One of the ways to evaluate the success of a project is to ask whether it stayed within its budget.

More Information on Nonprofit Accounting

Deciphering financial reports can be challenging. Don't hesitate to get someone experienced in bookkeeping to guide you through the process. If you or anyone in your nonprofit wants to find a CPA with expertise in nonprofit accounting who is willing to donate his or her services to your worthy cause, here are some suggestions on where to find one. Each of the following organizations also has helpful literature on nonprofit accounting issues.

Accountants for the Public Interest (API) is a national nonprofit organization that encourages accountants to volunteer their time and expertise to nonprofits. The services they provide range from assisting in tax preparation and establishing record-keeping systems to supplying budget and financial management advice. API has affiliates throughout the country. Its Internet site is quite helpful and includes a full listing of API affiliates. Contact API at Accountants for the Public Interest, 1012 14th Street NW, Suite 906, Washington, DC 20005; tel.: (202) 347–1668; Web site: www.accountingnet.com

Local accountants associations have outreach programs that provide information and assistance to nonprofit organizations. Ask your local accountants association for the name of its pro bono accounting coordinator and the areas in which the association offers assistance. If you need help in locating an accountants association near you, use the *National Directory of Volunteer Accounting Programs,* published by Accountants for the Public Interest (see the first item in this list).

To-Do Exercise 3.1 will help you to begin analyzing your organization's financial history with an eye to future fundraising needs and tactics.

TO-DO EXERCISE 3.1

Drawing Fundraising Ideas from Financial Data

Go to your organization's bookkeeper and get a copy of the financial statements for the last few years. See what the numbers were last year and the year before and the year before that. Get an idea of what the giving trends have been. Look at the income categories, not just revenue from contributions but revenue of all types. Then go a bit further. Do any of the income categories suggest fundraising ideas? If your organization has ticket sales, for example, find out how many subscribers it has. These people already support your organization in one way. You may be able to come up with a method to entice them into becoming donors as well.

Chapter 4

Breaking the Funding Need into Manageable Parts

AT FIRST GLANCE an organization's funding need may seem insurmountable. How do you get a grip on the dollars needed and take the first steps toward raising them? Constructing a realistic overview of your fundraising plan eliminates a great deal of confusion and anxiety. Although it is important to figure out in general terms where the contributions are going to come from, trying to pin down every donor all at once is not productive. The first step is to break your fundraising goal into manageable parts.

This process requires making contribution estimates by types of donor, by the activities used to raise the money, or by a combination of both methods, whichever best fits your organization's fundraising style. Whether your program is brand new or an established charity, you can design a working overview of your fundraising goal and how you will meet it. This overview funding plan is the base upon which your full fundraising plan will be built.

The overview process for existing nonprofits differs a bit from that for new nonprofits. If you are a fundraiser in a nonprofit with a giving history, you will take these four general steps:

1. Use the organization's giving history to create fundraising estimates. Identify traditional funding sources (by donor categories, fundraising activities, or both) and the percentage of total contributions typically received from each.

2. Estimate changes in giving behavior that can be expected this year compared to previous years.

3. Divide this year's funding need into parts, based on historical experience and adjusted for any expected changes. Assign each part to a donor category or fundraising activity category.

4. Ask what specific donors and fundraising activities are going to match up with specific funding needs. This is a brainstorming exercise that tests the assumptions used in earlier steps and helps make your overview reasonable and practical.

Use the Giving History to Make Fundraising Estimates

It is not unusual for a nonprofit organization to have a relatively consistent pattern of giving. A small number of individuals often contribute the bulk of a nonprofit's funding. For many organizations, as few as 10 to 20 percent of donors provide 70 to 80 percent of their funding. If this scenario fits your nonprofit, then your estimates of the upcoming year's contribution sources should be that a similar percentage of your funding will come from your group of top donors.

Within the top group there may be one large contributor who accounts for 10 to 15 percent of an organization's total philanthropic dollars. A handful more may bring in 20 to 25 percent. And the balance of donors in the top group may account for about 30 to 40 percent. That leaves 10 to 30 percent that will come from lower-level donors.

Such an arrangement of contributions is referred to as a *giving pyramid* (see Figure 4.1). A few major donors at the top of the pyramid account for a sizeable proportion of contributions and a relatively large number of donors at the base contribute a small portion of the total. There is an inverse relationship, in other words, between the number of donors in a giving category and the size of the funding they provide.

The giving pattern in Figure 4.1 may not be applicable to your group of course. For your giving pyramid use percentages that correspond to your

---

FIGURE 4.1

Giving Pyramid of a Typical Nonprofit.

Percentage of All Donors	Percentage of Funding
<1	10–15
3–5	20–25
7–15	30–40
20–30	5–20
50–70	5–10

organization's experience. Eventually you are going to put names next to these amounts, but first, you want to see this overview of what can be expected if history repeats itself, a reasonable assumption for stable non-profit organizations. Of course even gifts you count on need a fair amount of tending to be realized. Those steps are described in Chapter Ten. However, you will be in a better position to schedule specific fundraising activities once you have prepared the overview of your funding need.

Another way to overview your fundraising need is by program area. What are the costs of the specific programs your organization provides, such as services, educational events, exhibitions, or publications? The process of focusing on expenses can also stimulate ideas on how to package crucial but unglamorous costs, such as utility bills and custodial services, so they appeal to donors.

Yet another way to overview fundraising need is by fundraising activity, such as mailings, membership, and special events. In the example we are about to give, a PTA uses a combination of donor categories and fundraising activities to describe how it intends to fund an after-school program.

Nonprofit organizations with a history of raising funds can use that history to make their estimates. Nonprofits that are raising money for the first time do not have a giving history to base their projections on. They need to estimate their expenses, their funding need, from the ground up. Here is an example.

The PTA of a local grade school wants to provide an after-school program. One hundred of its members voted for the program. Expenses are budgeted at $35,000. The program is not expected to produce any income.

Two PTA members who strongly believe in the program have each offered to contribute $500 to the effort. They are going to look for two additional people to match their gifts, for a total commitment of $2,000.

It is decided by a fundraising committee that each PTA member is going to be asked to contribute or raise $100 in support of the after-school program. This is presented to the general membership, who approve it. If everyone participated (there are four hundred members) that would yield $40,000. But to be conservative, income from these contributions is projected at $10,000 (on the assumption that one hundred members who voted for the measure will make the requested contribution).

In addition, three PTA members have decided that they can best help this cause by organizing a benefit dinner dance. They form the nucleus of a committee for this purpose, and the committee decides on a barbecue and square dance theme. The goal set for the benefit is to raise a net $10,000.

Another event is scheduled for later in the year, a holiday bake sale. Sales are projected at $500.

At this point, the PTA fundraising committee takes stock. How much money still needs to be raised if everything succeeds as planned?

Four individuals contributing $500 each	$2,000
PTA member contributions (100 at $100)	10,000
Benefit	10,000
Bake sale	500
	$22,500

Amount outstanding: $35,000 –22,500 = $12,500

The PTA realizes it needs to go to the community outside the school for help. There are twenty small businesses in the town, two of which are banks. The PTA decides to ask each of the banks for $2,000 (for a total of $4,000). Before it does that, though, it will try to develop a groundswell of gifts from the other local businesses: two grocery stores, a hardware store, a dry cleaner, a bookstore, and so forth.

The PTA fundraising committee persuades the town newspaper to donate space so that the PTA can offer to acknowledge (with ads in a Monopoly board pattern around a big "Thank You") the local businesses that contribute to the community's after-school program, which now has an attractive logo designed pro bono by a local artist. A goal of $500 is set for each of five prominent local businesses (5 × $500 = $2,500), and a goal of $50 for each of the rest, apart from the banks (13 × $50 = $650).

The committee now has a plan to come up with $7,150 of the outstanding $12,500, but it is still short of funds. So it decides to run a phonathon and to be prepared to run a second phonathon if necessary. A group of ten PTA members will call every family in the school. They will try to get each one to give $5 to $10. The committee members estimate that 600 of the 1,300 families in the district will give, raising anywhere from $3,000 to $6,000 from the first phonathon. So they may not need a second one.

Estimate Changes in Giving Behavior

The next step for an established nonprofit is to factor in how this year differs from last year. Have expenses increased? Is the organization starting the year with money in the bank? If so, is that money more or less than the organization had last year? Is the organization fairly certain to receive any particular contributions or other revenues, such as income from multiple-year gift pledges?

Look again at what happened in previous years, not just at how much your nonprofit raised but from whom. If a donor's giving profile has dramatically increased or decreased, you may want to do some additional research before setting a giving goal for that donor. Answer the following questions to estimate donors' future giving plans.

• Which donors can be expected to *renew* their gifts? Which can be expected to increase (or decrease) their gifts? Has a donor's gift remained the same for a number of years? Has it increased by a certain percentage each year? This is not a science, but by analyzing past giving patterns, you can make your estimates more accurate. Write down the assumptions you are basing your estimates on. Do this for each major donor and donor group, such as corporations and foundations.

• Are you aware of any *pending cutbacks?* You want to stay abreast of changes at corporations. Their contribution budgets can shrink following mergers or business losses, and their giving guidelines can change in ways likely to reduce support to your group. Knowing early about cutbacks gives you a better chance to search for alternative funding elsewhere. For example, when government support was shrinking for cultural institutions, the new development director of a Los Angeles cultural center made sure her staff kept in touch with each government funding agency, and giving projections were adjusted accordingly. As a result the center was prepared early on to seek alternative funding to replace losses in government support. In addition, each year there will be some natural attrition of your nonprofit's individual donor base. If you can't compare this year's results with those of the previous two years, then assume that your organization will lose 15 percent of its previous donors and its donor income, which you will need to replace with new and increased gifts.

• What is the funding *growth potential?* A certain percentage of your donors, the ones that know and love your organization best, such as volunteers and board members, can be pretty much counted on to renew and over time to increase their gifts (that is, with proper care and attention). Look for a pattern of increased giving, and factor that into your giving estimates where appropriate. Say you have an individual whose first contribution to your organization was $1,000 and his second contribution was $2,500. From this pattern, you project his giving will continue to grow, but to be conservative you estimate his next gift at $3,000. That's a smaller increase than last year's, but without a commitment in advance from the donor, it is better to be conservative than to set your sights too high. Being overly optimistic in your projections can result in a huge shortfall.

If you have no giving history to go by, it's pretty hard to make estimates on how much you will raise except by going to potential funders and getting indications of interest and initial pledges for support. As you begin raising money you will put some flesh on your fundraising overview and be able to start gauging your chances of success more realistically.

With a new venture it's a good idea to get a few key supporters behind the effort before publicly launching the fundraising campaign. That way you can refer to their commitment and cite their support when asking others to join in.

What if your nonprofit is an established organization that didn't have to raise money last year but does now? That's a situation faced by some county public health organizations, for example. Until recently, they could rely on government funding to completely support their activities, but now they find they are facing reductions or cuts of important programs unless they can replace rapidly shrinking government grants.

If you are going from ground zero with your fundraising or need to replace a major funding source, try targeting a select group of individuals who are familiar with your work. Don't create unrealistic goals by expecting to have new funding in place overnight. Ideally, your organization will have six to twelve months to fund a new project or replace a major funding source.

Divide the Funding Need into Parts

To explain the step of dividing the funding need into parts, we go back to our PTA example. Because the PTA after-school program had no giving history, the fundraising committee had to accomplish part of this step earlier in order to identify its sources, as discussed in the example for step one.

Once the members of the PTA committee have completed their brainstorming about the potential donors they will solicit, fundraising activities they can organize, and the dollar amounts that can reasonably be expected from each, they write out the results in outline form, as illustrated in Exhibit 4.1.

Match Funding Parts with Donors

Let's say your fundraising goal is $100,000. And you have identified, as percentages, how much your top gift has typically been and how much your other top donors and lower-level contributors have given. You have

---

EXHIBIT 4.1

PTA After-School Program: Overview Funding Plan.

PTA Members	Fundraisers	Companies	Other	Total
Member requests: $10,000	Dinner-Dance: $10,000	Banks: $4,000	Bake Sale: $500	
Large member gifts: 2,000	Phonathon: 3,000–6,000	Ads: 3,150		
12,000	13,000–16,000	7,150	500	32,650–35,650*

Backup fundraiser: if the fall phonathon raises less than $5,350, do another in the spring.

---

estimated future contributions based on a review of historical giving trends and current donor information. Now you ask yourself, Who is going to fit into those giving categories?

At this initial stage of the plan, matching names with amounts is most constructive when done *with imagination*. It's a brainstorming exercise that tests the assumptions used in earlier steps and therefore helps answer important overview questions. How much increased funding must come from existing donors and fundraising activities to meet this year's goal? Can we reasonably expect these outcomes? Why? Do we need new donors? How many and in which categories? Should we consider new or additional fundraising activities?

After one community sports facility with a goal to build an Olympic-sized pool broke its funding goal into giving categories and specifically matched them to targeted donor prospects, one major prospect didn't pan out. So the sports facility's fundraisers went back to the drawing board, saying, "OK, we're still looking for one $50,000 gift and two $25,000 gifts. Whose giving profile fits those categories?" They kept going through that process until their goal was met.

If your organization had five $10,000 donors last year and you budgeted for five $10,000 donors this year, you will want to match names to those numbers. Ideally, at least two of them will be people who gave $10,000 last year. And then you may have a couple of people who gave between $5,000 and $8,000 last year and who have the interest and ability to do more. Most of your major prospects should have had a previous relationship or familiarity with your organization. At the time you enter prospective donors into your fundraising plan, you should have a strategy in mind for getting a gift from them.

Does It Have to Be Done This Year?

Some programs lend themselves to a flexible funding schedule. If yours does, then you can free yourself from meeting an annual fundraising goal. The Jewish Heritage Program at World Monuments Fund (WMF) has a budget of approximately $5 million for restoration of ten synagogues in Eastern Europe, Asia, and North Africa. But when do the funds have to be raised? At the end of this year? At the end of two years? As WMF raises the money for this important venture, it will do the work, even though the longer it takes, the more it will have to deal with increased costs in these countries, including inflation. Costs will change and the price of the project will go up.

An example of how flexible funding can work is WMF's Jewish Heritage Program, which has been active since 1988. As of 1997, a number of things have been accomplished. Early on, surveys were done and published on monuments in Czechoslovakia, Poland, and Morocco; and material was also collected on monuments in Syria. In 1992, after three years of research and evaluation, the Tempel Synagogue in Kraków, Poland, was the first site where restoration work occurred.

In this kind of fundraising, a track record of work accomplished can grow over time, and a reputation can become established that helps build funding. World Monuments Fund is an organization with a record of completing other projects, but progress continues only as funds are generated.

Keep Up with Changes

Changes in plan estimates will occur throughout the year. One corporate fund director keeps a monthly lookout for changes in the following indicators by comparing year-to-date results to previous years' numbers.

- Repeat donors: How much was given by how many donors? Were these numbers up, down, or flat compared to last year? What was the average size of each gift? How much was received in increased dollars?

- Recovered donors: How much was raised from donors who didn't give last year although they had given in previous years? How many donors were recovered? What was the average gift?

- New donors: How much money was received? How many new contributors were there? What was the average gift?

- Totals: How does the total year-to-date giving (repeat, recovered, and new donors) compare to last year's giving? How much remains to be raised before we reach our fundraising goal?

With To-Do Exercise 4.1, you can begin to get a clear picture of your nonprofit's typical funding patterns and the kinds of gifts you might reasonably seek as your funding need increases.

TO-DO EXERCISE 4.1

Creating an Overview Plan

Select the version of the exercise that matches your organization.

Exercise for an Organization with a Giving History

Based on your organization's giving history, create an overview, a picture, of how you would meet a funding need that is 20 percent higher than last year's. (For example, if your organization raised $100,000 last year from 125 donors and had one $25,000 gift, three $10,000 gifts, four $5,000 gifts, ten $1,000 gifts, and the remainder below $1,000 or $500, you would estimate the increases in level of gifts and number of gifts you would need to bring in $120,000.) Build a giving pyramid of fundraising targets based on the previous funding your organization has received. This exercise will give you an overview of your fundraising plan using historical data and will answer the question, How many gifts at what levels can we expect to receive if past giving patterns prevail?

Exercise for an Organization with a New Program

Take the sum total your organization needs to raise and break it down by the fundraising activities and solicitation strategies that you will use, such as cultivation events, grant requests, and major gift prospects (look at the PTA example in this chapter). Approach prospective donors to gauge their interest and enthusiasm in the program. Decide on the fundraising strategies you will use with these prospects and determine a reasonable financial goal for each. This exercise will build your fundraising plan from the ground up and answer the question, What fundraising techniques do we need to use and which prospects do we need commitments from, at these estimates, to reach our fundraising goal?

Part Three

Deciding Plan Inputs

Chapter 5

Creating a Core Communications Piece

FROM LETTER APPEALS and membership updates to phonathon scripts and benefit committee invitations, communicating with constituents is an ever-present necessity. That's why preparing a *core communications piece* is such an important part of fundraising planning. In order to attract contributions it is essential to present your organization clearly and in a compelling manner. Fundraising writing can seem a daunting task. By what method can you confront the blank page and create effective letter appeals? The answer to that is the subject of this chapter.

Think of your core communications piece as your *basic funding proposal*. There are several advantages to creating this core document and keeping it handy. First, creating the document yourself ensures that you stay in touch with the changing needs of your organization and with the justification (the case) for soliciting the gifts that fund those needs. Second, specific proposals can quickly be adapted from the basic one, which acts as a kind of checklist of facts, examples, and stories that you may wish to cite. Finally, a core communications piece is a handy subset of the organization's case statement.

Elements of a Case Statement

An organization's core piece for communicating with constituents is based first of all on the organization's case statement. The process of creating a case statement begins with defining the organization by considering questions such as

- What is the organization trying to accomplish?
- What makes the organization special?

- How much money does the organization or program need to raise?
- How will the organization evaluate its programs?
- What has the organization achieved?
- Who supports the organization now?

Answers to these questions establish what Henry Rosso calls an organization's "knowledge base" (Rosso and Associates, 1991, p. 40). Rosso divides this information into twelve categories: mission, goals, objectives, programs and services, staffing, governance, facilities, finances, planning, statement of needs, evaluation methods, and history.

These data are the raw material for the case statement. The result is a publication or a series of publications that explains why the organization exists, what it does, and whom it serves.

Much has been written on how to put together a case statement. We recommend the following articles:

Panas, J. "The Magic of Your Vision." *National Society of Fund Raising Executives Journal,* 1991, *16,* 53–56.

Taft, J. R., and Berendt, R. J. "Perfecting Your Case Statement." *Nonprofit Executive,* 1983, *2,* p. 7.

Walker, K. "Case Statement: The First Foot Forward." *Fund Raising Management,* 1995, *23,* 38–42.

Here we focus on how to use elements of the case statement to generate the steady stream of communications that are a regular part of a fundraiser's duties. We go over a two-step process for creating a core communications piece that begins with answering the questions asked by most funders. Once a fundraiser has been through this process, even grant applications need not get in the way of a good night's sleep. With the help of the case statement, by the end of this section you will be able to complete a boilerplate funding proposal such as a basic grant application.

The Donor's Point of View

It's important to remember that major funders receive thousands of requests for support annually. The way to stand out from the pack is to understand your donor's perspective and attend to it in your writing. Knowing a donor's interests is just as important as knowing what you are going to say. In fact addressing these interests is what shapes the most effective fundraising appeals.

Donors will be comparing your funding request with all the others they receive. They are open-minded about contributing to charities with similar missions. But in general they want to concentrate their support on the nonprofits that will have the most impact. Asked in a slightly different form, the six questions that help generate the case statement become these six questions reflecting specific donor concerns:

Donor Questions	**Donor Concerns**
What is this nonprofit trying to accomplish?	Do the nonprofit's goals fit in with my interests?
What makes this nonprofit's project special?	What distinguishes this nonprofit from other nonprofits that are doing the same thing?
What is it this nonprofit wants from me?	How much money does it really need? Does it have a project budget? Has it really thought out this request?
How will this nonprofit evaluate its program?	What progress reports will I get? How accurate will they be?
What has this nonprofit achieved?	How has it responded to similar challenges? How well will it follow through on its goals and objectives?
Who else supports this nonprofit?	What types of donors give now? Who is on this nonprofit's board, and how much do board members give?

Case Development and Support

Developing the answers to the first four donor questions helps you focus on the audience with whom you want to communicate. Developing the answers to the last two donor questions requires you to accumulate *case support*, the physical evidence that lends credibility to the answers to the first four questions. In a way the former show the organization's good intentions, and the latter provide information that supports the organization's ability to follow through on its intentions.

Donors want to know that their contributions will be well spent. They want to know *before* they make a contribution. We all know that past performance does not infallibly predict the future, but it does give donors a framework from which to look at your organization. That's why relevant excerpts from your organization's history of accomplishments can help donors appreciate your ability to accomplish the goals you set.

Generally speaking, the more recent your stories and examples the better. Your use of history will differ, however, depending on your organization. The "Venerable Art Museum" may have over one hundred years of accomplishments. Prospective donors can be impressed with its track record. The nearby "New Technology Museum," less than ten years old, will still have to work at getting donors to recognize its name. Although it won't impress donors with its longevity, it can make a case for the amount it has accomplished in a short span of time. Brand-new nonprofits need to cite the accomplishments of their executive director, board members, and other supporters in order to show that they can achieve their goals.

A Two-Step Process to Create Effective Appeals

Creating a core communications piece involves two steps:

1. Gather your ingredients. Answer the first four questions that address the concerns all donors have. Lengthy grant proposals not withstanding, answers to these basic questions will provide the core for most funding proposals you write.

2. Support your answers. Present true stories about your organization's accomplishments, mini-case studies that act as proof of your organization's ability to follow through on its goals and objectives. When appropriate, create more credibility by supplying information about who else supports the organization (see Chapter Six).

Gather Your Ingredients

We assume you have access to all the elements of your organization's case statement, most probably in the form of several documents that cover the twelve knowledge categories mentioned earlier. You have the mission statement, written materials on programs and services, and the relevant budgets. Given time to reflect, you could probably come up with phrases in response to all the donor questions. In fact, it would be helpful to do that now. Think of statements that express what you would most like to communicate about your organization. What would you like donors to remember about it? Take your time. There isn't just one correct answer to each donor question but many possible answers.

Expand on Your Mission Statement

Using elements of the organization's case statement will streamline the process of answering donors' questions. What your organization is trying to accomplish is reflected in its mission statement and organizational goals. The former addresses the societal needs that your worthy cause addresses. The latter grounds the philosophical statement with intended actions. Both help determine what makes your nonprofit distinctive and deserving.

Define Evaluation Tools

How many events will your nonprofit put on? What is the proposed schedule? What numbers and kinds of audiences are expected to attend? Determining organizational objectives involves putting due dates to goals and quantifying them. These measurable criteria can be used as the basis for accurate, honest evaluation of programs and services.

Use Your Project Budget

How much does your organization already have committed to its project? Where are you going to get the rest of the funds? How much do you want to ask from the donor you are writing to? Answers to such financial questions can completely redirect a communication. Accurate figures lend credibility and confidence to an appeal. Letter appeals do not always need to present the details behind your funding request, but you should be ready to supply and explain them upon request.

At this point, take the time to do To-Do Exercise 5.1, which will help you define the reasons people should give to your organization.

Support Your Answers

Of course, you don't want to send donors just a list of the top ten reasons to give to your worthy cause. You want to reflect your organization's personality, not just a group of dry facts. You want to point to relevant parts of your organization's history that prove that it can follow through on its mission, goals, and objectives.

The ingredients of your basic funding proposal will include positive statements about your organization, backed up by relevant examples and stories about its history. You want to select stories that involve prospective donors emotionally. Think about the Save the Children campaign. Every

TO-DO EXERCISE 5.1

Giving Donors Reasons to Support Your Organization

Answering Donor Questions

Write down two or three responses to the donor questions listed below.

For example, to show what it is trying to accomplish, a food bank might say, "We pick up unwanted food and deliver it where it's needed most," and, "We reduce hunger in an efficient way." Use descriptive phrases to highlight the most important aspects of your organization. Extend the answers when you can. What makes a nonprofit special, for example, is something it does. It may primarily put on chamber music concerts. But how many different ways could that appeal to a donor? Does the nonprofit regularly involve local schools? The statement, "We put on chamber music concerts," might be supplemented with the information that "children who participate in our in-school education program get free tickets to our chamber music concert series."

Later we will show you how to shape your answers for particular donors, but for now simply write down what you would like donors to know about you.

- What is your organization trying to accomplish? (What are its goals? Why are they important? Give them urgency.)

  _____

  _____

  _____

- What makes your organization's project special? (Describe what's distinctive about it. What makes it stand out from others that are similar?)

  _____

  _____

  _____

- How much money does your organization want? (What does it really need to complete its program? Be as specific as you can at this stage about how much is needed and why.)

  _____

  _____

  _____

- How will your organization evaluate its program? (Describe the procedure it will use? How will it measure success?)

  _____

  _____

  _____

ad has a picture of a ragged child in it. Seeing that forlorn young person standing barefoot strikes a strong emotional chord and makes the reader contrast the child's life with his or her own comparative well-being. We're not saying that you should always aim your message straight at the donor's guilt complex. The point is that pictures and stories can communicate emotionally as well as factually. Select stories that will make others *care* about your group. Paint verbal pictures. And of course, if you have a particularly telling photograph, use it.

World Monuments Fund brochures include side-by-side pictures of buildings before and after restoration. It's a dramatic effect. The impact of WMF's work becomes immediately and tangibly apparent. This is the impact you want to create with the stories you select to support your organization's work.

As you consider your answers to the questions in this chapter, begin thinking about the types of donors you want to reach. You want to motivate people to care about your organization. You want a positive response to your program. Charitable appeals that engage the intellect alone get responses like, "Sounds like a great cause. Good luck, but let me think on it; I'm overcommitted right now," instead of, "Count me in. Tell me how I can help." An effective way to begin to develop the communications that will convince your donors that your organization is worth caring about is to add interesting, heartwarming stories about your organization to your basic answers to the donor questions. Such stories can have a powerful effect, giving you a better chance of raising funds for your worthy cause. To-Do Exercise 5.2 will help you to identify some of your best stories.

Once you have selected some stories and examples in To-Do Exercise 5.2, you will need to tell each story in more detail so that it addresses four points, as the following story about a youth orchestra does. This orchestra doesn't just travel around the country playing great music, it builds audiences for its performances and for classical music. Audience building is an important aspect of what the orchestra tries to accomplish, and the story backs up the orchestra's claim to that accomplishment:

> In each of its cities, the orchestra sets up Concert Committees that include business, political, and educational leaders as well as local citizens. The partnership with the City of Dallas in 1993 became a model for working with Chicago in 1996 and will be used to shape a program in cities in 1999 and 2000. The orchestra's Dallas City Council worked with the Mayor, the Dallas Orchestra and scores of volunteers in mobilizing the city's resources, down to organizing buses so that city youth, senior citizens and handicapped—individuals who would not otherwise have done

TO-DO EXERCISE 5.2

Selecting Real-Life Stories that Illustrate Your Mission

For each answer you gave in To-Do Exercise 5.1, think about a story that illustrates it. Choose an event or series of events in the life of your organization that people will remember, that will stick with them.

As an example, consider the formula used by Covenant House, the largest privately funded child-care agency in the United States. It sends mailings to its donor base seventeen times a year, and each direct-mail piece mentions the Covenant House mission to provide shelter and service to homeless and runaway youth. Each mentions specific problems kids face that Covenant House knows about from personal experience: "kids who have run away from home, often from places hardly deserving to be called a home—kids who are abused, neglected, rejected and empty but yearning for fulfillment and, thank God, still having in their hearts that spark of hope that things can change." Every direct-mail piece centers on a specific real-life story that illustrates a problem Covenant House faces and shows how it addresses that problem. Sister Mary Rose, the organization's president, uses similar stories in her speeches, as she did in her 1998 commencement speech at Stanford University (www.covenanthouse.org):

Kenny came to Covenant House when he was just 17. In his initial interview, he refused to give us the name and phone of someone to call in an emergency. The staff asked me to talk to him. I explained that the only reason for wanting such a name and number was to call someone in a crisis. I said, "Suppose you go out and get hit by a truck and are in the emergency room, who am I going to call?" Kenny looked me straight in the eye and said, "Sister, if that happens to me, you just pray for me because there is nobody on the face of the earth who cares if I live or die." Can you imagine that? Can you imagine having no one who cares if you live or die? A young man just a bit younger than you are.

What makes your organization special is not only what it does but whom it helps and the manner in which it does so. Briefly identify the following stories:

- What real-life stories give testimony to your organization's accomplishments?
  _____
  _____
  _____

- What stories best illustrate what your organization is known for?
  _____
  _____
  _____

- Who are the heroines and heros at your nonprofit? What are their stories?
  _____
  _____
  _____

so—were able to attend concerts. Fifty-two families hosted musicians in homestays and attended the concerts. Our extensive preconcert press campaigns helped publicize performances. Volunteer groups such as "Hospitality Dallas Style" helped out, raising money to pay for the dinners and other expenses of hosting the group, and assisted in audience development. The result—The Meyerson Symphony Center was packed with capacity crowds that thoroughly enjoyed the performances.

Here are the four points to consider when coming up with your own stories.

1. Be clear about the goal of the story. The story in the example has a goal of showing how the orchestra builds audiences.

2. Describe obstacles faced by the organization. The story in the example says that audiences for classical music are unavailable to broad-based audiences.

3. Describe steps taken to overcome the obstacles (this is the heart of any story). The story in the example shows how the orchestra worked with local community groups. It formed a Concert Committee to mobilize city resources so that people "who would not otherwise have done so" were able to attend. Families that hosted musicians attended concerts. Press campaigns helped publicize concerts. And prestigious volunteer groups raised money and involved themselves in audience development.

4. Present a picture of the result. The story in the example tells readers that "The Meyerson Music Center was packed with capacity crowds that thoroughly enjoyed the performances." The phrase "capacity crowds" offers a measurement of the result.

Look further at the wording of the story about the orchestra. It's visual. It's active. We are left with an impression that every neighborhood and community group was included. You can practically hear the buses taking people to the concerts. Active verbs are used throughout. Programs are "shaped" and resources "mobilized," with the result that the concert hall was "packed."

What's the concept behind the story? The orchestra works with its concert communities to build enthusiastic audiences. That could easily be an answer to the question, "What makes the orchestra special?"

The phrases you wrote to answer the questions in To-Do Exercise 5.1 and the stories you suggested in To-Do Exercise 5.2 to back those phrases up work together. They make potent ingredients for a charitable request because you have taken a compelling reason to give to your program and supported it with real-life excerpts from your organization's track record. Now, in To-Do Exercise 5.3, you can work on the presentation of your materials, modifying your stories and making them more active.

What If I Have Writer's Block?

So what's the difficulty with finding answers to the questions donors ask? Nothing, if you're one of the few people who get excited about sitting down and writing. Many people, though, have a reluctance to do so. Let's be honest; most of us avoid it like the plague!

And if you are one of those people for whom writing is a chore, here's another way you can go through this process. Ask someone at your institution, or even a friend who is not part of your institution, to go through this exercise with you by interviewing you. Sometimes it's easier to express yourself orally to an audience than to write out what you want to say. So give the person the list of phrases you want to use (from To-Do Exercise 5.1), and also show her the four story points. Ask her to play the role of someone who's a prospective donor but doesn't know much about you or your organization. Your goal is to answer this donor's questions and get her interested in your institution. Have a tape recorder up and running during the interview. Afterwards, listen to the

---

TO-DO EXERCISE 5.3

Engaging Donors with Your Organization's Stories

Take your stories from To-Do Exercise 5.2 and develop them using the four story points. A good story is one that demonstrates that your organization can and will follow through with its goals. Your stories will address donors' unspoken concerns. You will not merely be asking for support. You will be proving what your organization can do for others with donor support.

Remember, each story needs to communicate these four points:

1. A goal the organization wanted to reach.
2. The particular obstacles that had to be overcome.
3. The means used to overcome the obstacles and solve the problem.
4. The results of the organization's actions, stated as concretely as possible.

Start with the first question donors ask: What is this nonprofit trying to accomplish? Once you have found and structured stories that support your responses to that question, go on to the next question, until you have covered all the questions. At the end you will have generated the basic ingredients for all your charitable requests.

tapes, transcribe them, and then edit them. You may be surprised how articulate you can be.

Be Positive

There are many reasons people support nonprofit organizations, some altruistic and others self-serving. People may be looking for recognition or the prestige of being associated with a cause, or they may strongly identify with the nonprofit's mission. People also give to respond to societal needs, to capture opportunities, to advance the human spirit, or to serve a purpose larger than themselves.

No matter what inspires each of your donors, the case you make for support needs to be positive. Financial need is simply not a strong enough motivation for support. There is nothing inspirational or exciting about needing money. And being broke is not necessarily synonymous with being ethical or honest. It may be synonymous with unsound financial management, which is death to a funding request. In an era when donors want every dollar to count, inability to manage your financial affairs is a land mine. So never make financial need the central thesis of a funding request.

Use Your Ingredients to Fill out a Grant Application

Once you've prepared your ingredients, grant applications will no longer look daunting. You won't have to stay up nights wondering how you will satisfy all the application requirements; you will already have done your homework.

Take a look at the National Network of Grantmakers (NNG) Common Grant Application (Exhibit 5.1). This standard form is now on the World Wide Web. Over fifty foundations and corporations have adopted it.

This form was developed to simplify the application process for nonprofit organizations and their funders, and nonprofits and grantmakers throughout the country have developed similar regional forms. To find out if a common application form has been adopted by corporations and foundations in your area, check with your regional grantmaking association. Here are some associations that offer common application forms on the Internet and that you can reach through links on the Foundation Center Web site (www.fdncenter.org):

Association of Baltimore Area Grantmakers

Coordinating Council for Foundations (Connecticut)

Delaware Valley Grantmakers (Pennsylvania)

Grantmakers of Western Pennsylvania (hosted by Carnegie Mellon University)

Minnesota Common Grant Application Form

National Network of Grantmakers

New York/New Jersey Area Common Application Form

Rochester Grantmakers Forum

Washington Regional Association of Grantmakers

Wisconsin Common Application Form (hosted by Marquette University)

Take a moment to review the NNG Common Grant Application or one from your part of the country. You should be able to take some comfort when you look at it. There are no surprises now. Having completed the exercises in this chapter you will be armed and ready to tackle this application. After you have reviewed the application form, complete To-Do Exercise 5.4.

EXHIBIT 5.1

NNG Common Grant Application Cover Sheet and Common Grant Application.

(Please feel free to make copies of this form.)

Organization name: _____

Date of application: _____

Address: _____

_____

Telephone number: _____ Fax number: _____

Director: _____

Contact person and title (if not Director): _____

Grant request: $ _____ Period grant will cover: _____

Project title (if project funding is requested): _____

EXHIBIT 5.1 (continued)

NNG Common Grant Application.

Type of request :

__ general support   __ start-up costs   __ project support

__ endowment   __ capital expenditure   __ technical assistance

__ other _____

Total project budget (if request is for other than general support): $ _____

Total organizational budget (current year): $_____

Starting date of fiscal year: _____

Summarize the organization's mission (2-3 sentences):

_____

_____

_____

Summary of project or grant request (2-3 sentences):

_____

_____

_____

NARRATIVE (maximum of 5 pages)

Describe your organization

1. Problem statement: What problems, needs, or issues does it address?
2. Briefly describe your organization's history and major accomplishments.
3. Describe your current programs and activities.

Describe your request

1. (If you are requesting general support, you may skip this bullet.) If other than general operating support, describe the program for which you seek funding, why you decided to pursue this project and whether it is a new or ongoing part of your organization.
2. What are the goals, objectives, and activities/strategies involved in this request? What is your timeline?
3. Who is your constituency? (Be specific about demographics such as race, class, gender, ethnicity, age, sexual orientation, and people with disabilities.) How are they actively involved in your work and how do they benefit from this program and/or your organization?

EXHIBIT 5.1 (continued)

NNG Common Grant Application.

4. If you are a grassroots group, describe your community. If you are a state, regional, or national organization, describe your work with local groups, if applicable, and how other regional and/or national organizations are involved.

5. Describe systemic or social change you are trying to achieve.

ATTACHMENTS (supply everything checked below by the funder sending this form)

Evaluation

Describe your plan for evaluating the success of the project or for your organization's work. Who will be involved in evaluating this work—staff, board, constituents, community, consultants? How will the evaluation results be used?

Organizational Structure/Administration

1. Briefly describe how your organization works: What are the responsibilities of the board, staff, volunteers, and, if a membership organization, the members?

2. How representative are these groups (board, staff, etc.) of the communities with which you work? Please outline general demographics of the organization.

3. Who will be involved in carrying out the plans outlined in this request? Include a brief paragraph summarizing the qualifications of key individuals involved.

4. Provide a list of your board of directors with related community and employment affiliations.

5. Organizational chart showing decision-making structure.

Finances

1. Organization's current annual operating budget. (See attached budget format.)

2. Current project budget, if other than general support. (See attached budget format.)

3. List individually other funding sources for this request. Include amounts and whether received, committed, or projected/pending.

4. Most recent completed year's organizational financial statement (expenses, revenue and balance sheet), audited, if available.

5. A copy of your IRS 501(c)(3) letter. If you do not have 501(c)(3) status, check with the funder to see if they are willing to fund through your fiscal sponsor, or are willing to exercise expenditure responsibility. Additional information may be required to do so.

Other Supporting Material

1. Letters of support/commitment (up to three)

2. Recent newsletter, articles, newspaper clippings, evaluations, or reviews (up to three)

3. Recent annual report

4. Other _____

_____

Source: *National Network of Grantmakers, 1717 Kettner Boulevard, Suite 110, San Diego, CA 92101; tel.: (619) 231–1348; fax: (619) 231–1349; Web site: www.fdncenter.org/onlib/cga/nng.html*

TO-DO EXERCISE 5.4

Creating a Basic Funding Proposal

Take a turn at filling out the NNG Common Grant Application Form shown in Exhibit 5.1, using the tips provided in the remainder of this exercise. These tips are keyed to the sections and numbers of the Common Grant Application questions. Next to each application question, we suggest using the response you have already prepared to a specific donor question or using other work you've already done in this book. Take those prepared materials and plug them into the application. Then review what you have done and edit it so that it flows smoothly.

Tips for Plugging Your Answers into the NNG Common Grant Application Cover Sheet

Total project budget (if request is other than general support): Give your organization's program expense budget (Chapter Three), which also supports your answer to the donor question, What is it this nonprofit wants from me?

Total organizational budget (current year): Give your organization's operating budget (Chapter Three).

Summarize the organization's mission: Use your organization's mission statement.

Summary of project or grant request: Use your answer to the donor question, What makes your organization special? Indicate the problem your organization addresses (organizational mission and goals), the actions the organization takes to address the problem, and who benefits (use your answer to the donor question, What is this nonprofit trying to accomplish?).

Tips for Plugging Your Answers into the NNG Common Grant Application

NARRATIVE (maximum of 5 pages)

Describe your organization

1. Combine your organization's mission statement, goals, and recent history related to accomplishing the mission and goals.

2. Use your answers to the donor questions, What has this nonprofit achieved? and, What makes this nonprofit's project special?

3. Use the organization's summaries of programs and service descriptions and your answers to the donor questions, What are you trying to accomplish? and, What has this nonprofit achieved?

Describe your request

1. Use the organizational or program mission statement and your answers to the donor questions, What is this nonprofit trying to accomplish? and, What has this nonprofit achieved?

2. Use your preparatory material for answering the donor question, How will this nonprofit evaluate its program?

TO-DO EXERCISE 5.4, continued

3. Describe whom you serve; use your organization's mission statement, goals, and objectives and your answers to the donor questions, What makes this nonprofit's project special? and, What is this nonprofit trying to accomplish?

4. Use your answers to the donor question, What makes this nonprofit's project special?

5. Use your answers to the donor question, What is this nonprofit trying to accomplish?

ATTACHMENTS

Evaluation

Use your answers to the donor question, How will this nonprofit evaluate its program?

Organizational Structure/Administration

1. Provide responsibilities of key staff, volunteers, and members and describe how they work together to accomplish the aims of the organization.

2. Compare the demographics of the organization to the demographics of the population you serve.

3. Provide short résumés of key staff.

4. Provide a list of members of board of directors.

5. Provide the organizational chart.

Finances

1. Provide the current annual operating budget (Chapter Three).

2. Provide the current program, or project, budget (Chapter Three).

3. Use your answers to the donor question, Who else supports this nonprofit?

4. Provide a financial statement, if available (Chapter Three).

5. Provide a copy of your organization's 501(c)(3) letter from the IRS or a copy of the umbrella (or parent) nonprofit's 501(c)(3) letter along with a letter from that umbrella organization stating you are authorized to use it.

Other Supporting Material

1. Provide up to three letters of support/commitment (see Chapter Six).

2. Provide up to three recent newsletters, articles, newspaper clippings, evaluations, or reviews (see Chapter Six).

3. Provide a recent annual report, if available.

4. Other (see Chapter Six)

Now look over your work on this exercise and take a moment to appreciate what you have accomplished. Remember this: different funders' forms for funding proposals will have different formats, but they all require the same or similar answers. Now that you have filled this form out, you've got a leg up on all the rest.

Chapter 6

Selecting Case Support Materials

CASE SUPPORT BOILS DOWN to credibility; it is what makes people believe that your organization will accomplish its goals and objectives. Case support is so important to successful fundraising as to be obvious, but it cannot be taken for granted. Often donors are not the direct recipients of a nonprofit's assistance, and so they must rely on evidence that the nonprofit organization they give to is living up to its claims. A successful fundraising campaign requires the ability to communicate to potential donors that the organization is legitimate, that its worthy cause or the need for its service is significant, and that it is the best qualified to provide that service.

To communicate this message, you need to plan which case support materials to gather and how to present them in a cohesive, attractive package. Some items, like a list of your board of directors, you already have. Other pieces you are going to pull together in this chapter. Once you do that you may be surprised to find that your case support materials communicate credibility more strongly than a paid advertisement would.

The Need for Case Support

If your prospective donors haven't heard of your group, how do you catch their attention and express that you are worthy of support? How do you get known for the important work you do? These days you have to show *evidence*, verifiable proof that you are legitimate. Having your financial statements reviewed or audited by a certified accountant helps; accounting numbers can be analyzed and compared. A 501(c)(3) letter from the IRS is proof of your organization's nonprofit status. But you need more.

You need to convince donors that you do good work. That can seem a distant second in importance to actually carrying out the good work, the mission, of your nonprofit; it can seem an energy drain, taking manpower and time away from the effort necessary to provide services. However, it is difficult to get funding if people don't know what your organization does and that it does it well. Think of the American Red Cross helping a community after a river flood, organizing assistance, setting up shelter, and providing food for the afflicted. The direct assistance the Red Cross provides is what helps people; *that* is what's important. Yet even the Red Cross constantly updates the public, through ads, news articles, and direct mail, about what it does. As well known as it is, even the Red Cross will have difficulty attracting the funding it needs unless it keeps people informed about what it does and why that work merits support.

How can a grassroots nonprofit get the word out about its programs? After all, the American Red Cross is nationally known; it has sponsored advertising and gets pro bono support from the Ad Council. It maintains a department entirely devoted to public relations to ensure that the public knows about Red Cross activities. But be assured there is plenty you can do even without a large budget and a public relations staff.

The Press Kit:
Your Donor Information Packet

Your initial task is to develop a standard set of *public relations* documents for your worthy cause that you can put in a folder and send out. Such a folder, loaded with credibility exhibits, is called a *press kit*. The term comes from the set of materials that organizations hand out to reporters at press conferences. When a company unveils a new product, for example, it hands out a press kit that contains marketing brochures, specifications, press releases, and other material the company wants the public to know. Similarly, one press kit that a nonprofit needs is a collection of materials that can be distributed to media and to donors and prospects to inform them about the nonprofit's legitimacy, credibility, and worthiness in relation to its cause—its case support.

What the items in this press kit and donor information packet actually say will of course depend on the message you're trying to get across to your donors. But whatever the individual message, most kits will have all these types of documents:

- Fact sheet on the organization

- Letters of endorsement

- Recent news articles

- Short résumés of key staff

- Information about the board of directors

- Information about your donors

- Evaluation information

- A copy of the organization's 501(c)(3) letter from the IRS

- The operating budget and financial statement or audit from the previous year

The last two items have been discussed earlier. In this chapter, we focus on how you can prepare the first seven items.

Fact Sheet on the Organization or Specific Project

An organizational fact sheet is a combination of headlines, short sentences, paragraphs, and bulleted lists that communicate the essential information about your organization. Your fact sheet should include a description of the most important aspects of your organization as well as some or all of your answers to To-Do Exercise 5.1. The following list itemizes what you should include in this single-page document:

- Organization name, mailing address, telephone number, e-mail address, Web site address

- Major endorsement or quote (from well-known personality, if you have one)

- Brief organizational history and description of programs

- Mission statement

- Key facts, such as who heads the organization

- Facts that make your organization stand out

- Size of the organization and scope of its programs

Letters of Endorsement

You need to let the media and donors know that there are people who will speak up for your organization and say, "These people are doing good things." At first blush you may wish for a famous media personality to come forth. Or how about a national hero?

Well, there are national heroes and there are local heroes. Local is usually better because they're the ones that make a difference in your community. We were reminded of this at an assembly when a man who had counseled teens for twenty-five years got his turn at the podium. "I don't care what you all think of what I'm about to say," he told the kids, "I'm going to say it anyway. Forget about Michael Jordan. Forget about Madonna. The heroes that matter in your life are right here in this room; your teachers and the volunteers that are making this program happen. They are the real heroes. The others may be fine athletes and performers, but they have no power to directly affect your life in the way that these men and women will, who dedicate themselves to helping you kids, days, nights, and weekends."

Sure, it would be great to have a respected, nationally known celebrity behind your group, perhaps a former First Lady who attests to the singular importance of your organization's work. After all, you are competing with a million other nonprofits and you need help! But if the latest box office star or a former president isn't on your organization's board, don't worry. Get the people who do know your nonprofit to give their heartfelt testimony about how they or their families have benefited from it. Their words may be your most powerful tool. Let them speak and register their praise.

Endorsements from Constituents

If an outside expert knows and respects your program, by all means, ask him or her for a recommendation, but also consider this example. A Chicago youth program solicited a local utility company with a history of supporting programs for inner-city kids. Good news: the corporate contributions officer had grown up in one of the neighborhoods served by the program. Bad news: the program had been around twenty years, and she had never heard of it. The program director knew he had trouble. "What can we do to catch their attention?" he wondered.

Organization staff brainstormed about finding some recognized expert who would endorse the after-school and summer youth program. Then they decided to ask their constituents, people who already knew the program. They went to the parents of children in the program and asked them to write a few lines about how their kids had benefited. In addition, two of the volunteer counselors, both local policemen, wrote about why they volunteer for the program. They signed their letters with their title, "Volunteer Counselor," and their professional status, for example, "Lieutenant, Chicago Police Department." One young man who had gone through the program from age six through sixteen now serves as a counselor. He added his heartfelt letter to the growing pile of endorsements.

Everyone wrote in his or her own words. The list of positive statements from the parents took up a full page. It looked like the back cover of a best-selling novel. The comments were testimonials to the good things that the program does for kids. The name, address, and telephone number of each person quoted was typed in. An interested donor could check the information. That kind of openness inspires credibility.

The community youth program got its first corporate grant. And being from a reputable company, the contribution added to the organization's credibility (a benefit we discuss further later in this chapter).

Endorsements from Outside Experts and Others

The Civic Orchestra of Chicago runs a free music education program for community groups and schools. Members of the orchestra work in a wide range of activities, including teaching, coaching, and giving lecture-performances. Throughout the year they provide free concerts to outside community members of all ages. The community groups that participate as audiences have written glowing letters about the program. Their letters get shown to prospective donors and are included with program funding proposals.

Endorsements can come in other forms than letters. For example, a known celebrity might make a public service announcement (PSA) on a radio station about your worthy cause. Endorsements can also be made in person. Amy Rosenfeld runs The Working Playground, an organization that works with at-risk teens through theater arts. In her program, Breaking the Barriers, she gets teenagers to write about their feelings and express themselves through acting.

Amy asked for funding from a small foundation that focuses on crisis intervention programs for youths. Along with the funding proposal, she sent letters from two public school principals praising her project (Exhibit 6.1). The people on the foundation board still had questions about it, so Amy requested an opportunity to meet the board (you can do that with smaller foundations), and she asked if she could bring with her a principal from one of the schools where she worked. The foundation board members were so impressed with what the principal had to say about Amy's program that they funded the project.

Another factor in Amy's favor was that she had gotten the board of education to support her project. You can imagine how hard it is, with declining school budgets, to get money from the school system—especially

---

EXHIBIT 6.1

Sample Endorsement Letter.

The Institute for the Arts & Technology
444 West 56th Street
New York City, NY 10019

Terry Born   Codirectors   Juliana Rogers

November 8, 1994

Dear Ms. Rosenfeld:

    I am writing to let you know how pleased I am with the work you have been doing with our classes at the Institute. Breaking the Barriers is a program which enhances attendance and encourages higher quality performance by engaging students in activities promoting concentration, imagination and collaboration via a vehicle which uses students' personal experiences.

    One of the reasons I am especially pleased with the program was the way in which you enabled us to tailor the program to existing interests of students and faculty at the Institute. One of our staff members has been wanting to combine Soap Opera writing and acting with the video program for several years. You have inspired students to come to school excited in anticipation of the days they will work with you. As a teacher of theater for over 15 years it gives me great pleasure to support your work and I anticipate a long relationship with you and your program.

                                                  Sincerely,
                                                  Terry Born, Codirector

---

for a program that's not mandated. The board of education grant gave the program another leg to stand on; it provided legitimacy. Amy needed both the board of education grant and the principal's faith to convince the foundation of the worthiness of her program (Amy Rosenfeld, personal communication [board meeting proceedings]).

Endorsements from Renowned Sources

As described earlier, the World Monuments Fund (WMF) runs a program that identifies and restores important Jewish monuments. Its press packet includes a letter from Simon Wiesenthal, the renowned Holocaust writer. After visiting one of their restoration sites, the Tempel Synagogue in Kraków, Poland, he sent WMF a letter praising its efforts. Because of his reputation, Wiesenthal's endorsement added credibility to the program. The synagogue, a mute survivor of one of history's greatest tragedies, is now, due to the efforts of WMF, once again available to the community and the world.

Don't Wait for an Endorsement—Draft It!

Occasionally you may need to draft an endorsement for an important supporter of your program. One nonprofit working on an important restoration project in Charleston, South Carolina, wanted to evidence the local government's support. The mayor is a hearty supporter of the project, and the organization felt it was important to have his written endorsement. However, the mayor's office didn't know what the nonprofit really wanted him to say and so asked if the nonprofit staff would draft something. The mayor then signed this letter, changing only a few of the words. The nonprofit got the endorsement faster than it would have otherwise and now can include it in the press kit and donor information packet.

Complete To-Do Exercise 6.1 at this point, starting to think about who might endorse your organization.

Recent News Articles

Newspaper and magazine articles about your organization can build the public sense of its legitimacy and keep its worthy cause in the public eye. They provide tangible evidence that your concert was well received, that your research institute is considered tops in its field, or that your organization is well run and efficient. Keep clean copies of these articles on hand. Store the originals separately so you can make more copies as needed (we assure you that copies of copies can get so fuzzy that you'll wish you had the originals!).

Recent articles usually carry the most value, but keep a historical file of news clippings and other records of media attention. In the 1980s, an episode

---

TO-DO EXERCISE 6.1 °

Share the Good Things People Have to Say About Your Organization

Positive references—what people outside your organization say about you—give a stamp of approval that is essential to your organization's effort. Identify and list the strongest outside voices likely to support your organization's statements about what it does and how effective it is.

1. _____

2. _____

3. _____

4. _____

5. _____

of the *Bill Cosby Show* featured a young inner-city football team much like the Brooklyn Skyhawks, a nonprofit football program for children aged seven to sixteen located in Brooklyn, New York. A few of the Skyhawk players were actually in the show, and people are still fascinated when they hear this. They always say, "Really? How'd they end up doing that?"

Short Résumés of Key Staff

You need to tell people who's running the place. Your press kit should include one-paragraph résumés of key staff that address the following three points:

Accomplishments and recognition. Ideally, you will have noteworthy things to say about the staff of your worthy cause, especially the executive director and program directors. Donors like to know the facts that show staff are qualified and special. What degrees do they hold in their fields? Are they members of professional organizations? Have they received awards or other recognition? Given a speech? Published articles or books? It's good to update these staff profiles periodically and list new accomplishments. (Put staff accomplishments in your newsletter too.)

Qualifications. People like to evaluate information against a standard. They expect certain kinds of expertise from people running certain programs. Social workers are expected to have a master's degree in social work. Private schools tend to inform constituents of faculty who hold postgraduate degrees. So mention formal staff qualifications and say how long staff have worked in their fields. If some staff don't have the usual education but have gained the kind of real-world experience that may let them surpass someone with a degree, let donors know that.

Dedication and commitment. Let donors know about the extra efforts staff and volunteers make to get the job done. Effort and sacrifice reflect commitment. Brooklyn Skyhawk coaches, for example, are all professionals, such as police officers and firefighters, who juggle their work schedules in order to keep their weekends and evenings available to work with their teams. These men make unseen sacrifices so they can be there consistently to coach the kids. The Skyhawk kids do not know all that their coaches do to make it to practice; they just know they can count on them. Some people say role modeling is the strongest teaching there is. These men are role models where few exist. Can you think of a stronger way to express to those kids that somebody cares about them, that they matter, or to express to potential donors that the Skyhawks are doing work that other people consider very important?

Information About the Board of Directors

Nonprofit board members are legally entrusted with overseeing the organization's management, so naturally donors want to know something about them. How involved are they? What percentage of the board contributes money personally to the organization? Contributions are shorthand for commitment. Each organization should have internal guidelines that protect confidential board member data, including who has access to this data. For your press kit, draft a one-page piece (honoring the privacy constraints determined by your nonprofit) that lists the board members, with two or three items about each one—where he works, how long he has served, particular specialties or interests—anything that expresses *the board member's* credibility and commitment. If 100 percent of the board members have made donations, be sure to say so.

Tell people more about any prestigious board members, including honorary ones. If your nonprofit is little known, the involvement of a high-profile board member can make a difference to prospective donors. The first ladies of Russia and the United States are honorary cochairs of the American Russian Youth Orchestra (ARYO). In 1995, Hilary Clinton and Naina Yeltsin cochaired the orchestra's tour, as did Barbara Bush and Raisa Gorbachev in 1993. A signed letter of endorsement from each first lady, on official stationary, is always included in ARYO's press kit. For prospective donors who have never heard of ARYO, the involvement of such prestigious political personages offers instant credibility and a feeling that this nonprofit deserves a look.

Information About Your Donors

Like horse racing fans and stock market investors, donors to nonprofits like to back a winner. They like to give to organizations that already have support. If proof of worthiness attracts contributions, it's reasonable to assume the equation works the other way as well, that donations demonstrate worthiness. A list of major donors will be scrutinized by others as the organization's charitable pedigree.

Grants by foundations or individuals show an organization is well regarded. The assumption is that these donors did their homework before they gave. Some foundations, such as the Mott Foundation of Flint, Michigan, are known to do quite a bit of homework before approving a grant. Their grants carry a particular cachet of legitimacy.

If a grant is large enough, it merits a press release (press releases are described later in this chapter). Monsanto and the Monsanto Fund together awarded a $3 million grant to the Missouri Botanical Garden for the Monsanto Center, a new state-of-the-art research center that houses "the world's most active and productive botanical research staff and contains [the staff's] Herbarium and Library" and that expects to attract "hundreds of scientists and scholars from around the world to study in St. Louis" (www.mobot.org/MOBOT/pr/index.html, press release #98032). News coverage of this grant and the Monsanto Center brought the Missouri Botanical Garden to the attention of people throughout the country and the world.

Obviously if someone gives money to your organization, you will list her as a contributor. But what if someone gives your organization a computer, a painting, or another kind of gift? Isn't this person a donor too? Sure she is. Create a list of gift-in-kind donors. Add them to your donor list under their own category. Stores that donate equipment, for instance, should be listed as donors, also businesses that donate space in their buildings. Their names give your nonprofit credibility. Their donations act as an endorsement, showing they think highly of your organization.

Evaluation Information

Program reviews can boost an organization's legitimacy. In your press kit, you can show accomplishments in terms of numbers of people served; numbers of subscribers, members, or visitors; per person costs; the percentage who drop out; and success ratios. Museums are always mentioning the number of people who visit them ("2.2 million visitors have come through our doors this year"). They also measure how many people come to a particular show or event. Another form of evaluation for them is what outside experts or the news media say about them and their exhibits. Nonprofits can quote positive media statements to support their numerical results.

A Seattle settlement house has been working with teen mothers, helping them get their high school equivalence degree. How many young women have stayed in the program and gotten their GED degree? What is their dropout rate? How many have gotten pregnant again while participating in the program? These are all measures the settlement house uses to evaluate its success.

How do you rate your organization's achievements? You may never have thought in these terms. If not, don't worry, there are plenty of nonprofits evaluating themselves these days. In order to get an impression of how they do it, take a look at the literature of some organizations similar to yours. Call them up and ask them to send you an annual report, and some recent newsletters.

You know the level of services your organization started out providing and what level it supplies now. That's one comparison you can measure. But it's always nice to have a standard benchmark to measure yourself against. How much better did your program do than the norm for similar programs? In the stock market, for example, a mutual fund may be up only 5 percent, but if the overall market is down, then the fund is doing well because it's doing better than the standard performance benchmark. If the stock market were up 10 percent, then that same fund result would be considered poor compared to the benchmark. Similarly, there are benchmarks against which one can measure what is going on in society at large.

Rehabilitation programs track their participants over time. The success rate is higher the longer participants stay sober and the longer their changed behavior lasts. Say that after a number of people go through a program to stop drinking, 15 percent of them immediately go back to drinking, and 35 percent start drinking within six months. It's hard to tell if that's good or not unless we are also know what the average success rate is for all such programs.

Find a standard, a benchmark, against which to measure your program activities compared to the activities of other nonprofits in your field. Present as many facts as possible in comparing the results of your program with other nonprofits' results.

You also know what goals you started with. Compare how your organization is doing on achieving its planned results. Be honest. If your organization fell short, determine why and explain what added knowledge it will take into account or what course of corrections it intends to take next time.

There is nothing wrong with getting advice from large funders on how they would like to see a program like yours evaluated. Be sure to have your own plan ready though, as it may be easier for funders to evaluate your organization if you provide a draft plan to work from. In that way, you will make the most of their time and yours. Use the funders' advice to redraft your evaluation procedures, then add this revised draft to your press kit.

Finally, numbers may not lie, but by themselves they don't impress donors. Even if you are talking about huge numbers of people served, you need to explain the importance of the figures you cite in your press kit. Saying that 100,000 people benefit from your organization does not have the same effect as saying that, for example, you have provided arts instruction for 100,000 children who don't have arts programs in their schools. When you are writing up an evaluation, give heart to the numbers.

How to Organize Your Press Kit Materials

Get a file drawer ready. Empty it out. It's time to put together your press kit files. Keep boxes of photocopied news articles nearby. Have separate folders for the different categories of material: press releases, fact sheets, letters of endorsement, program evaluations, and so on. A major accomplishment will be organizing these case support materials in one place to make them easily accessible.

You will probably find more evidence validating your organization than you thought there would be. Some things, like your board of directors list, you already have. Other pieces, like endorsements or articles, you're pulling together.

Once they are filed in one place, you can pick and choose from them. When it comes time to send out funding proposals, information to donors, or press releases, you will be able to easily pull out the appropriate set of attachments to support your request. Like the team leader in the old *Mission Impossible* television series, you will select the backup materials that will best get the job done, whether your mission is raising funds from a particular prospect or obtaining attention from certain media.

To-Do Exercise 6.2 will take you through the first steps of assembling a simple press kit and donor information packet.

TO-DO EXERCISE 6.2

Putting Your Press Kit Together

Take the first step toward putting a press kit together for a prospective donor. Decide on a central place for your press kit files so you can have easy access to them. Using this chapter, make a list of the items you need. You may still need to do some of the following:

Complete the profile of your organization or project.

Think about endorsements. In To-Do Exercise 6.1 you considered which organizations and individuals it would make sense to ask for letters of recommendation. Start collecting these letters of praise about your organization from different sources. For example, if you're doing a project in the public schools, get endorsements from the principals and teachers of those schools. Ask the kids to write about how they have felt about participating in your program.

Choose the best published articles on your organization.

List your major donors.

When you have collected these items, put them in a press kit folder, perhaps a presentation folder with pockets. Put in a copy of your most recent newsletter. Personalize it with your organization's mailing label and the prospective supporter's name.

The Press Release

What if *Newsweek* and *Time* magazine or the TV news shows haven't gotten around to covering your organization or specific project yet? Don't wait for them. Create your own *press release* that spreads the word about your nonprofit's worthy cause.

Two hundred years ago, Benjamin Franklin knew how important it was to draft press releases and send them to local papers. It was a standard practice he said he followed *before* asking others for contributions: "Previous however to the Solicitation, I endeavored to prepare the Minds of the People by writing on the Subject in the Newspapers, which was my usual Custom in such Cases" (Franklin, 1964, p. 199).

As in Ben Franklin's time, reading about a nonprofit in a newspaper or magazine lends an added degree of credibility. Draft your press release from the perspective of what you want to get across and *what will catch the eye of your local news agencies*. Give your article a timely or seasonal angle so that it won't get filed away. For example, the Missouri Botanical Garden is savvy about getting articles printed in St. Louis papers—it emphasizes seasonal attractions as they blossom. Look at your worthy cause from an editor's point of view. What are the readers' interests?

Also write press releases to capitalize on noteworthy grants or donations you receive. That's positive community news and the local press will want to know about it, so will donors when you are soliciting them for support.

Once you have written a press release, call publications and other media to find editors and reporters who cover the same causes and interests your nonprofit exists to serve. Send your press release, and your press kit to them. But also put all your donors and prospects on the mailing list.

The American Museum of Natural History's new dinosaur hall got plenty of press. Many people heard about the new hall but had it made them more willing to give money to the museum? It is true for institutional donors as well as individuals that unless they experience a nonprofit's new endeavors themselves *or hear about them from a trusted source*, they continue to think about the nonprofit in their old way. For the Museum of Natural History, that meant the *sleepy* old way.

We were with an eighty-three-year-old friend when we first walked into the redesigned dinosaur hall. All of us were impressed at how informative, thought provoking, and beautiful the new hall appeared. We all felt that after more than a decade of installing uninspiring, aesthetically static exhibition halls, the museum had taken a major step and that it deserved support in this effort. Some people believe donors tend to support causes that emphasize their dire straits and the money they need to survive. But in fact people like to support winners, organizations that can prove they succeed at what they say they do. The American Museum of Natural History had proof that it was a winner with its new dinosaur hall. Its fundraisers had good news to share. Their task then became to make sure that the news was heard, to make sure that the perceptions of donors and prospects were kept up to date.

The Importance of Regular Communication

An absolute necessity for building credibility and validity is *staying in touch* with the people who support you and the ones you are cultivating for contributions. The more they get used to you, the more familiar you become. This is important. Fundraising after all isn't really about numbers, it's about people. Even if your organization regularly sends out newsletters, at some point you will want to contact prospective supporters personally. Such contacts build trust. Donors learn they're not just names on your direct-mail list. And they are able to ask questions about the organization they might not otherwise ask, about its finances, how its program is rated, or whether the founder still serves on its board. With your organization's case support materials selected and organized, you will be able to keep all donors appropriately informed about all the reasons the organization's cause is worthy of their support.

Chapter 7

Recognizing Potential Donors

IN CHAPTER THREE you gathered as much factual data as you could in order to estimate what contributions your organization could raise from different categories of donors. Now it's time to get specific about who those donors are going to be—which new prospects have the highest chance of contributing to your worthy cause and which current supporters could substantially increase their gift amounts. Without a schedule of research activities as part of your fundraising plan, you may allow individuals who have the ability and interest to become major donors to slip through the cracks. Nonprofits often have prospects who have the financial means to be major donors, but because their current contributions are relatively small, these prospects receive only mail solicitations and are never personally contacted. Nonprofits also typically have previous donors who are still interested in the organization's work but who have fallen off the contact list, perhaps because their contributions lapsed for a time. In this chapter we describe how to chart the information your organization needs to

- Increase the number of individuals who contribute to your institution

- Increase the average gift individuals make

- Find major donors

Understanding Who Your Best Prospects Are

Who participates in your organization's functions? Who donates time or money to your cause? Who has had a previous relationship with your nonprofit? Who has been served by your nonprofit? Look for relationships that lead to people who are familiar with your organization, who care about it, and who may very well want to contribute to it.

The best gift prospects are people who are already involved with your organization. That's one of the most powerful concepts in fundraising. In fact fundraising consultants rarely find a donor who isn't already linked to the organization. Instead, they help you recognize the potential that you may not have known was there, and help you maximize that potential.

Undoubtedly there are people whom you should be talking to who don't know your worthy cause, but chances are *you can be introduced to them through your current supporters.* So before you go looking for outside contributors, take a good look at who's already on your team. It's a basic premise of this book that your best prospects are already connected to your organization, and we employ it here to construct a base of donors and prospects most likely to support your worthy cause.

We are also going to talk a lot about matching the interests and financial ability of prospects with the activities of your worthy cause. That can be challenging, particularly when you are doing it for the first time. However, once you have been a fundraiser for a few years you will begin to accumulate a great deal of information about prospective donors that will make the process easier. To get an idea of how this can work, consider some hands-on fundraising techniques used by Sanky Perlown.

Terry met her in the late 1970s when Sanky was hired to design a direct-mail fundraising campaign for the American Museum of Natural History. This was before computers were in common use in offices, and to prepare for the series of large mailings, Sanky stayed late at the museum—separating out from the mailing lists the names of people whom she recognized from her consulting experience as potentially large donors.

On the one hand, pulling their names limited the likely results of the direct-mail campaign. On the other hand, it revealed buried treasure—individuals who should be personally cultivated—not sent "Dear Friend" form letters, no matter how cleverly constructed. The museum did deal with those people more carefully, and as a group they substantially increased their gifts, thanks to Sanky.

Because of her more than twenty years of experience working with nonprofit institutions, Sanky could rapidly recognize the names of potentially large donors. She didn't need to look people up in giving directories or on donor lists of other organizations. Until someone computerizes those kinds of skills, the rest of us will need the help of supplementary sources to help figure out the major contributors waiting to be discovered in our own backyards.

Identifying the Natural Donor Base

There are three major categories in your organization's natural donor base—*active supporters, previously active supporters,* and *prospective supporters*—along with an additional category of *suspects* (see Figure 7.1). Each category will answer the question, *Who already has a direct or indirect relationship with your worthy cause?*

Active Supporters

You will find most of your active supporters in four categories: donors, volunteers, employees, and constituents.

Donors

Who supports you with contributions now? Give those people attention because, in our opinion, your best prospect for a gift is someone who has recently given to your organization.

It is estimated that between 10 and 20 percent of a nonprofit's donors provide over 50 percent of its contributions (see Chapter Four). Your active individual donors expect to be kept updated about your work and can make up the bulk of your contributions. A major World Monuments Fund

FIGURE 7.1

Network of Individuals Most Likely to Provide Support.

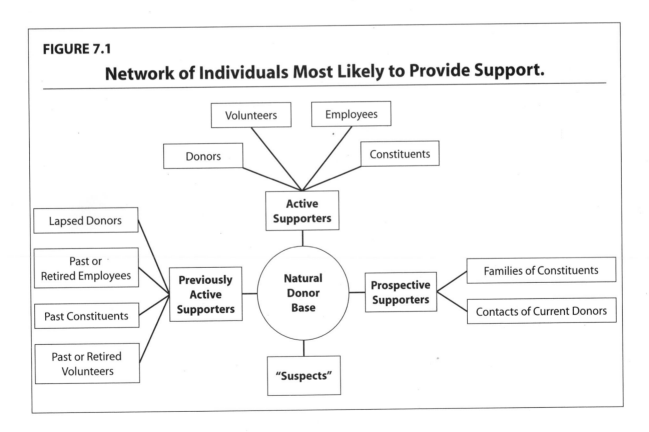

donor, for example, started out with a modest gift to the fund's Jewish Heritage Program. With the proper attention his contributions grew to over $100,000 a year.

Volunteers

People who invest time and effort volunteering for your worthy cause have made a visible commitment to it. The tasks they carry out are often essential contributions in themselves, which is one reason why volunteers get overlooked as prospects—they have already given time and effort. Another reason is that staff assume volunteers know the organization so well that it must be self-evident to them that a fundraising campaign is under way and that they would give if they could. Do not be misled by this kind of reasoning. Be sure to ask volunteers for contributions. Most people don't give until asked, and these individuals are prime prospects. A stunning 90 percent of volunteers contribute financially to the nonprofits they work for (Hodgkinson and Weitzman, 1994, p. 30).

Members of your board of directors are a special class of volunteer. Their leadership position in the organization means that their donations will be closely watched by other prospects and will set the tone for the fundraising campaign (see Chapter Nine). Bard College, for example, has attracted several board members who never attended the school and yet have given generously. In addition to providing operating support, major gifts from these board members have founded an institute of economics, established a graduate decorative arts program, and built a new gymnasium complex.

Employees

Don't forget those who work for you. Program and administrative staff, past and present, know what your organization needs and what it does better than anyone else. Long time staff often form special ties with their institution that go beyond merely picking up a paycheck. There have been several instances, for example, in which long-standing curators have given the American Museum of Natural History substantial sums of money.

Constituents

Who directly benefits from what you do? Who attends your programs? A constituent is anyone who has used your service, past, present, *or future* (for example, the student who will enter your school this fall is already your constituent). If your organization puts on concerts, check your subscriber list, your ticket buyers. Your audience consists of people who pay money to see and hear these performances; they *enjoy* what you do. In addition to being concert-goers they can become contributors. If you run a school, keep records not only of your students and alumni but also others who benefit from the school, such as groups who rent or use your facilities for after-hours activities. People participating in your programs have a relationship with you.

If you work for a social services agency, soliciting current beneficiaries for support is problematical. The beneficiaries of Save the Children, for example, are poor young children dependent completely on the kindness of others. Such organizations seek contributions from society by appealing to an overall charitable instinct, saying, "These children are human beings like us; we should all care." But even in social service organizations, sometimes you will find individuals who once directly benefited from the agency and later became able and interested to repay that kindness.

In 1920, the Washington Square Fund provided a home for unwed mothers. Times changed and the demand for its services diminished as other agencies took over, so the home was sold. The fund used the proceeds to become a nonprofit foundation that now supports youth crisis intervention programs. The Washington Square Fund does not seek donations in any way, yet people have sent them in. Unsolicited donations have come from women no one in the current organization knows. Members of the board believe that these donors once had a close relationship with the fund's home; they either worked, volunteered, or were residents for a time. These unsolicited angels remembered the home and wanted to show their appreciation for the work that went on there or their support of the women served.

Take a broad view of your nonprofit's constituents. An arts performing center, for example, has many constituents, for example:

- Members: these constituents can be further identified by membership category, such as young leadership, family, or senior.

- Audience: a list of subscriber names and addresses can be maintained. To take advantage of the organization's less established relationship with single-ticket buyers and people accompanying subscribers, post a sign near the box office inviting them to join the mailing list. Leave name and address cards (and pencils) next to a drop box.

- Performers: no one knows the challenging financial condition of an arts organization better than its performers. They are open to reasonable participation in benefit performances and in-school programs that further the prospect of future performances.

- Students and their families: teachers can be enlisted to be on the look-out for relationships with current students and alumni and with their families that could assist the fundraising effort.

We suggest that you take a moment here to identify your organization's constituents, as outlined in To-Do Exercise 7.1.

Previously Active Supporters

You should approach everyone who has done anything positive for your worthy cause in the past, even if you haven't heard from the person recently. These people may be inactive and easily overlooked, but they once had a stronger connection with your organization. Their inactivity now doesn't mean they don't care or don't have the ability to give. The reason you haven't heard from them may be as simple as "I didn't know you needed me." Include the following people in your natural donor base:

- Lapsed donors

- Past or retired volunteers, including board members

- Past or retired employees

- Past constituents, including alumni you haven't heard from recently and past members

Strong relationships can wilt if not attended to. There's an alumna who says she loves a private school we know of, but for thirty years no-

---

TO-DO EXERCISE 7.1

Organizing Your Constituent List

Consider each of the different groups that use the services of your nonprofit. Make a list of them. Don't leave any constituents out, because later on (in Chapter Ten) you will be learning how to ask them for money.

1. _____

2. _____

3. _____

4. _____

5. _____

body gave her any attention. The woman comes from such a wealthy family that she could build a new wing for the school without blinking an eye. At first the headmaster asked, "How can we ask her to support us after neglecting her for so long?"

Such situations are embarrassing and unfortunate, but they needn't be regarded as fatal. In this case, the school's intention is positive now, and just because previous employees at the school were neglectful, no one should presume to know how this alumna feels about her alma mater. Don't let fear or embarrassment stop you from reconnecting. As it was at this school, it is good news to both sides when an old friendship is rekindled.

Prospective Supporters

If the first rule in finding donors for your worthy cause is to look at who is already involved with your organization, the second is that you don't want to miss anyone with a possible link to your group. Approaching friends and close associates of those who know and love your organization and its cause is the way to creatively gather prospects. When contacted, such people have usually already heard of your organization, often have good things to say about it, and are open to give.

Two indirect relationships in particular can pay big dividends:

• Relationships with family members of people whom your organization has helped and of volunteers and employees. Sarah Seaver helped with the public relations effort for the American Russian Youth Orchestra's 1993 and 1995 tours. Her father, baseball hall-of-famer Tom Seaver, was invited to become involved and eventually hosted a charity softball match between the student-musicians (mixed teams of Russian and American players). It was fun for the musicians and added a celebrity to the ranks of the orchestra's supporters.

The more you have done for your constituents the stronger the feeling that those close to them will have for your organization. Family and friends of those who have been helped through a health crisis or a drug or alcohol dependency problem, for example, can be grateful and appreciative of a program even though they did not go through the program themselves. A classic case of raising funds from indirect relationships is the cultivation and solicitation of parents of currently enrolled students. In these days of tough budgets, that includes parents of public school as well as private school students, as all parents are getting more involved with providing support.

- Relationships with people connected to current donors. A development director we knew was planning a trip to Chicago to raise money for his nonprofit. He had a donor whom he thought had Chicago connections, so he started to network by calling her up. She said she didn't have Chicago contacts who could help but that a friend of hers did. He called her friend, and she gave him a big list of family foundations to contact. (He also quickly realized that the friend would make an ideal donor, and so began a cultivation process with her too.)

He took her list to the director of a Chicago foundation that had previously supported his charity. The foundation director had regularly dealt with the people on the family foundation prospect list. He would not host an event for the organization, but he did vet the list, supplying an address, telephone number, and a contact person he knew at each one of those foundations. Through this networking, the development director wound up with a very detailed list of sixteen foundations that he could take the next steps with.

Suspects

As you hunt for prospective donors, it can be useful to write down descriptions of the types of people you believe would be interested in your worthy cause *if they knew about it*. These suspects don't have a current relationship with your institution, but you perceive a possible match, probably because of something you have heard or read about them. If you don't come up with an introduction through someone already on your team, stay on the lookout for another way to reach these individuals. Once introduced to a suspect, explain to the person why he or she might be interested in your organization.

Another development director we know once found a major donor through a magazine article. The woman profiled in the article was an up-and-coming mover-and-shaker in our friend's community, and the development officer learned from the article that she worked at the same bank as one of his board members. The board member wrote a letter of introduction for him. The development director followed up on it, went to see her, and she became a major donor and fundraiser for his organization.

Now is the time to bring your current donor list up to date, as described in To-Do Exercise 7.2. This exercise will also get you started on selecting specific fundraising methods for specific donors.

TO-DO EXERCISE 7.2

Strengthening Your Donor List

Collect information on who is giving to your organization now in order to create or update your current donor list. Then look at all your different gift sources. You may find some people who have given generously but aren't on the list! Plan a strategy of how you're going to research, cultivate, and solicit them. Schedule when you're going to do it.

Chapter 8

Tracking and Evaluating Prospective Donors

ONE OF YOUR FUNDRAISING GOALS is to build a network of supporters with whom you can easily communicate. In order to easily reach people connected to your nonprofit, you have to plan how you will keep track of them. Smaller nonprofits can create this necessary database by hand. Other organizations should consider generic database products or specialized software designed to track donor information. This chapter goes over basic record-keeping needs and alternative systems, so that you can plan out a record-keeping system that's right for your group.

The Importance of Accurate Donor Records

Well-maintained donor giving histories can be invaluable. A review of a donor's records may open up interesting questions such as why her giving level has suddenly increased or why she once gave much larger gifts than you are receiving now. One new development director was told to concentrate on finding new donors. "Don't bother going to the contributors on our old donor lists" she was told. "We've already done everything we can with them." Well, it's always worth taking a fresh look. And in this organization's case there was one lapsed donor on their list, who, with the right kind of attention, came back in as a $10,000 contributor.

This happens even in well-run nonprofits. Why? Perhaps somehow a name doesn't get on the computer program, or a check goes through a different institution before getting credited to the nonprofit. One charity we know has a close relationship with a foundation. Some of the charity's donors send in their contributions through the foundation. Because those contributions are deposited and recorded at the foundation, sometimes vital donor information isn't recorded by the nonprofit. Once a $50,000 donor giving through the foundation didn't make it onto the charity's donor list!

The Basic Prospect Profile

It's essential to maintain accurate donor records. In the old days fundraisers scribbled donor information on 3-by-5-inch notecards. We remember a development director who used to drive us crazy with his detailed donor cards. But he was right. He was a real stickler for updating every piece of contact information and letter solicitation that his major prospects had ever received. This was before computers in offices, and we had to do it by hand. With computers in most offices now, few people use cards, though donor software input screens have been designed to look like them, with a place for the donor's name, address, and giving history; a status report, and a follow-up plan.

The larger the donor, the more information you want to record. For major gift prospects, be sure to include the following:

- Name: maiden name, any nicknames, and the person's preferred name (how he wants to be listed as a donor).

- Various addresses: current home and business addresses and any seasonal homes, along with all telephone, fax, and cellular phone numbers; also make space for e-mail and Internet addresses—more and more people have them.

- Spouse's name: if the spouse has the wealth, note that along with information on its origin and composition.

- Place of work: company name, job title, secretary's name, *and whether the company matches gifts*.

- Complete giving history: dates when the person gave and what he gave for.

- Contact person (solicitor): name of the person in the organization or on the board who has primary responsibility for developing the prospect and asking him for money.

- Communication: copies of letters you have sent to the donor, and at least for the current year, notes about what you have asked the donor for, donor responses, and copies of all acknowledgment letters sent.

- Your plan for further fundraising from the donor.

In addition, keep a record of important background information on the donor. What are his interests? Are there ways the donor is willing to help in addition to giving money, such as making introductions to other prospects and helping you approach them for gifts?

Describe the donor's overall relationship with your organization. Who first introduced him to the organization? Are the donor's relatives or other friends involved? What professional groups does the donor belong to? What other nonprofit groups is he affiliated with?

Has the donor contributed with gifts other than money? Did he donate a valuable item to last year's auction? Note that on the donor record. Does the donor bring bags of clothes to the thrift shop? Let you hold a square dance fundraiser in his barn? Write down anything about the donor that shows a direct interest in and commitment to your organization.

What to Think About As You Computerize

If you are using or introducing computer programs to help your organization's fundraising, you need to consider finding the appropriate software, ensuring accurate and full data input, and keeping certain materials in hard-copy form.

The Right Software

Choosing software to assist your fundraising efforts can be challenging, and the number of software packages available only makes it more so. Nevertheless, depending on how large your donor base is and how many categories it's divided into, you may find a fundraising program helpful. Before you go looking, it's a good idea to prepare a list of features you require. Then talk to several software vendors with *prospect and donor tracking program* software packages and test-drive their programs.

Certainly your record system should be able to produce a variety of standard reports and lists for use by staff and volunteers, including

- Prospect profiles and research

- Donor giving histories

- Mailing lists and labels

- Tickler reports for scheduled contacts

- Reminders of pledges

In addition to ensuring that the system you buy will do all the things you need it to, you should take these steps during the software selection process:

TO-DO EXERCISE 8.1

Filling Out Prospect Profiles

Fill out a prospect profile like the one supplied here for every major donor or at least your top five donors.

Prospect Profile (Confidential)

Name:

Residential address, phone, fax, etc.:

_____

Contact at [worthy cause]:

Business information:

Financial net worth/assets:

Family information:

Education:

Professional and community affiliations:

Giving interests:

Giving history to [worthy cause]:

Other interests and background:

Additional addresses and telephone numbers:

- Ask for local references and visit them to see the system in action.

- Find out where the support and training come from. Local support is much less expensive.

- Ask about the cost and quality of annual updates. References are a good source of objective answers here.

- Remember that software is and should be an evolving product. Ask the vendor about the direction in which the system is developing.

Accurate Data Input and Access to Data

Once donor information is centralized it's easier to access and modify it and to create reports from it. However, computerized reports are only as good as the data that are input. Accurate data input is essential to making a constituent database program useful. However, prospect and donor tracking programs are simply not as easy to operate accurately as one might initially think. Moreover, it can be difficult to find development assistants who can both input constituent data accurately and make the decisions that are needed along the way to ensure that the data are correct. If you find someone qualified, hold onto him or her. This person is a gem!

Keeping constituent data updated is a task you need to factor into your fundraising plan. It is really a team sport. Everyone needs to get involved, as in this example. When a staff member at one nonprofit was generating an acknowledgment letter and asked the development director's assistant if he knew the address of a donor who liked to receive his mail at his place of work, Bank of America, the assistant replied, "Why not just send it to Bank of America's main office?" It was explained that the bank owned a lot of buildings! Rather than send the letter to an address where it might be delayed or even lost, a phone call was made, and the correct Bank of America location was found and entered into the donor's record.

Constituent data input is a live process. Data must be input into the computer after a gift is received, for instance. The envelope comes in, is opened, and a check comes out. There may or may not be a letter. At times all you receive is a check. In either case it is normal to find that several decisions need to be made to correctly enter the gift and constituent data.

Complications can start just looking the person up on the system—essentially answering the question, Has this person given before? Say Jane Smith sent in $100, and there is no record of her on the system. Should a new record be created? Not right away. She may be on the system together with her spouse and under his name, John Smith. You might recognize the donor and know she has a history with your nonprofit, but what if a data entry clerk or assistant who has less experience with the organization is doing the input? To avoid duplicated records and accurately store all Jane Smith's gifts in one place, the assistant has to understand the importance of looking at other information, such as the address on the check, in order to find, for example, that the organization has a donor named John Smith listed at that address and that his record lists Jane Smith as his spouse.

What if the $100 comes in from a trust on a bank check with no other reference? This is not as unusual as it sounds. An inexperienced assistant might enter the trust as a new constituent when in fact it is just the vehicle through which a donor made a contribution. A person with more development experience would realize that it is essential to attribute the gift to the person who actually made it and that it might take a few phone calls to the bank to find out that Jane Smith controls the trust that made the gift. In this case the gift should be primarily credited to her, as she decided to make it.

What happens if the trust does get listed as a constituent? If the error is not caught, for example in the mail merge process, then the gift acknowledgment or any further solicitation will be sent to a lock box address at the bank, with very little chance that Jane Smith will receive it.

So what kind of qualifications should you look for in data entry staff? Whom do you want inputting your donor information? The more development experience the person has, the better. Barring that, some business experience is helpful. Ideally, you want somebody with a logical, curious mind, someone who, if he can't find a donor one way, will try two, three, or four other ways. When you have this kind of staff, even if Jane Smith is listed under John Smith, she will be found and her gifts properly recorded.

In addition to ensuring accurate data input, you need to be sure you have access to all the data that could help you in your fundraising effort. You need to be sure you can obtain all the relevant lists in your organization, perhaps through a computer network. What can happen in a rapidly growing nonprofit is that various offices begin to maintain their own contributor, prospect, and contact lists, with the result that the fundraising office may not have access to some of its best prospects. Years ago, for example, the American Museum of Natural History development office did not have access to subscribers to the museum publication *Natural History Magazine*. Subscribers were associate members of the museum, and the membership and development areas were run separately. How do you upgrade a member to become a donor? Ideally such subscription lists and membership lists will be available to your development office.

Similarly, the people managing a hospital's volunteers will maintain their own lists, but the fundraising office needs access to the volunteer lists so that these likely prospects can be solicited for contributions.

When fundraisers are working with these lists from other areas of the organization, it's not unusual for someone to point out something like, "Oh, my gosh, that's the wife of the president of the local bank. We know them." Or, "Look at this; I know this woman's family is independently wealthy. She donates her services but maybe she never thought of donating money. We need to ask." Encourage that kind of synergy by gathering the lists of people connected to your organization into a central location or a donor-prospect database.

When Hard Copies Are Helpful

Fundraisers don't have to keep as much hard copy these days as they did before they had computers, but a computerized donor record is no substitute for a separate file folder on each major gift prospect. Say you sent seventy-five letters to people identified as friends of a charitable project. Some of them had a history of giving to it, and some didn't. You're not going to stick a copy of each letter in all seventy-five of their files. But at the beginning of the file *for that project,* you would note there was, for example, a September mailing, and attach a list of everyone who got that letter, along with a copy it. If there were enclosures, such as an RSVP card, put samples of these items in the file also. Also note on each person's computer record that she received a solicitation mailing on that date.

Personalized letters should be kept in each major donor's file folder, along with relevant articles and research on that donor. Now that almost everyone uses a computer system, even copies of personalized letters often are not put into the hard files. When a file folder looks empty, go to the computer screen. From the folder it might appear that a major donor didn't receive a letter for two years when actually she received several mailings.

A note should go into a donor's file any time she is contacted by the development office, a board member, the executive director, or a friend of the organization. That way you have a record of the developing relationship and the plans you have made, and you can more easily determine the next steps to take.

Finally, all copies of letters that donors send when they make a gift should be in their respective files, along with the acknowledgments your organization sent.

Keep Track of Them So You Can Track Them Down

Alumni publications at colleges and universities have a goal of never losing an alum. They pay special attention to updating their mailing lists so that no alumnus or alumna ever misses a copy of the magazine. Whether the alum sends a change of address card or not, the publications office gets the forwarding address and reroutes the magazine.

Moreover, when it comes to fundraising, many schools have a broad definition of alumnus and alumna. Graduating is not a requirement to be solicited for money! In fact, the way some schools go after alumni for gifts, it seems that virtually anyone who ever spent a day on campus is contacted. As a result, many multimillion-dollar gifts have come from former students who did not receive a degree, but who have been diligently tracked and solicited as part of the alumni family.

To-Do Exercise 8.2 is your opportunity to begin your own top prospect file folders.

A Method of Evaluating Prospective Donors

Because you don't have the luxury of spending a lot of time with individual prospective donors, learning about them gradually, you need a method for evaluating them. Once you have established a method, you can plan out how much time to devote to each—which donors come first and how much effort you should spend on the others. This section of the chapter presents a quick, reliable evaluation and ranking system that will help you more efficiently cultivate and solicit the prospective donors you have identified.

Essentially, you need to measure three prospect qualities. We call them the 3C's:

- Capacity: assess each person's ability to help your organization financially. If the person gives modestly now but has substantial means, you can develop a plan to encourage him or her to build the level of giving.

TO-DO EXERCISE 8.2

Starting Top Prospect File Folders

Take your prospect profiles for the five top prospects (To-Do Exercise 8.1), and start file folders for each. Put in recent letters and any supporting or interesting material you found in your profile research.

- Commitment: review each individual's giving history with your organization. Your top prospects are people who are currently giving and have expressed interest in giving larger gifts. Also determine which donors have given consistently year-in, year-out. Small regular gifts can be a strong indication of commitment to a nonprofit's funding.

- Connection: review the strength of the individual's links to your organization. Who knows the prospect? How well? Is the person a volunteer? A graduate? A member? These links are the most important characteristics because they are the ones you can influence to increase prospects' interest and involvement in your nonprofit.

Another Look at the Giving Pyramid

It is not necessary of course to measure these prospect qualities for every donor. In Chapter Four we went over the concept of the giving pyramid, which displays the inverse relationship between the number of donors in a giving category and the total contributions those donors provide. A few major donors at the peak of the pyramid often generate a sizeable portion of total dollars raised, whereas the larger number of donors at the base of the pyramid provides the smallest proportion of overall funding.

Figure 8.1 illustrates the giving pyramid for a typical nonprofit, but supplying somewhat more detail than the example in Chapter Four so you can see more easily how to use these giving categories to prioritize donors. This nonprofit contacted nearly six hundred individual prospects to generate a total of $100,000. And as Figure 8.1 illustrates, slightly more than one-third of all its donors (55 out of 155) gave 92 percent of that total. Any organization's current top prospects are people who have given be-

---

FIGURE 8.1

Detailed Typical Giving Pyramid.

Gift Categories	Prospects	Donors	Average Gift	Percentage of Total Funding
$20,000	2	1	$20,000	20 percent
5,000–20,000	12	4	6,000	24
1,000–5,000	60	20	1,500	30
500–1,000	120	30	600	18
<500	400	100	80	8

fore. These 55 donors who gave $500 to $20,000 apiece are critical to the success of this nonprofit's fundraising, so it would focus on them in the coming year, and it would solicit the remaining donors and other prospects with techniques that do not require time-consuming research.

How to Measure Capacity

Once you have identified your most likely top donors, you are ready to measure the 3C's for each of them, beginning with capacity. You want to know how much each major prospect can contribute to your organization, but what are you to base your estimates on? After all, you can't get copies of donors' tax returns. And your giving pyramid doesn't tell anything about donors' capacity to give. It's possible that donors of mid-level ability gave larger amounts than wealthier donors did. The difference is attributable to each individual's commitment and connection to the organization. The top donor is certainly giving meaningfully, but how does the gift amount relate to her financial ability?

Fortune and *Forbes* magazines annually report on the nation's wealthiest people. Check these magazines if you think you have board members or other prospective donors who would qualify or are prominent enough. What about those not quite as rich? See whether your prospective donors are listed in *Directors and Executives, Who's Who in America,* or the other widely available reference books mentioned later in this section. Lexus/Nexus is an online service that is searchable by individual names. Your library may have access to it. If not, contact the Foundation Center library nearest you (see the Appendix).

In addition to checking published information sources (including news articles and on-line sources; see the Appendix), you can infer a lot about donors' wealth from where they live, the clubs they belong to, and the kind of jobs they hold. Do they drive his and her Acuras? Do they own multiple homes? We know one affluent lady who told us that she and her husband would pay more in taxes than it's worth for either of them to work. How wealthy does that make them? Are their assets worth $20 million, $100 million? We don't know exactly, but clearly she and her husband have the ability to give and to give generously. Make a note in the file of such donors and go on to the next.

When your prospective top donor is a board member, take a look at the biographical information you have already collected from board members. For both board members and other prospects, look at their known contributions to other causes, material you glean from news articles and on-line research. At theater performances, look at the list of contributors in the program guide. See if your board members or other donors are listed. Request the annual reports of nonprofit organizations and colleges in your area. Check their donor lists as well. Of course, if any donor has a family foundation, you can see what that foundation has supported and how much it has given in the past by looking at its IRS Form 990 tax return. Foundations' 990s are public documents; you can find them at Foundation Center libraries.

Research Tools for Individual Prospects

Here are some published research tools, available in many libraries. Ask your librarian about local directories also.

Reference Works

Dun & Bradstreet's Directors & Executives and *Standard & Poor's Register of Directors & Executives*. Both give names of prominent businesspeople and their place and date of birth, current position and company, and other associations.

Owners and Officers of Private Companies. Gives data on 100,000 executives from nearly 30,000 private companies.

Taft's Guide to Private Fortunes (vols. 1–3). Gives information on the interests and fortunes of over 2,200 individuals.

Taft's Major Donors. Gives data on over 16,000 individual major donors.

Who's Wealthy in America. Lists information on about 100,000 wealthy people.

Who's Who in America. Gives data on influential Americans. There are many specialized *Who's Who* volumes (for example, *Who's Who in American Law*, *Who's Who in Finance and Industry*, *American Women*).

Periodicals

Business Week

Chronicle of Philanthropy

Fortune

Forbes

Local business journals

Local newspapers

National newspapers

   New York Times

   Wall Street Journal

How to Measure Commitment and Connection

Eventually, you want to select methods to cultivate and solicit everyone on your donor lists, but first you want to select out people who should be dealt with individually. Knowing prospects' financial capacity is one way to do this. Knowing their commitment and connection to the organization is another way. Commitment measures participation, financial and otherwise. Connection speaks to an individual's existing relationships to your worthy cause.

Previous gifts evidence commitment. Look again at that relatively small group of donors who supply the bulk of your organization's funds. What is each donor's giving history? Which donors are consistent givers year after year? Refer to the linkages you assessed in identifying potential donors (Chapter Seven). What are each prospect's existing relationships to your worthy cause? How many constituencies does each prospect fall into? Is she a past employee, volunteer, member, or grateful client?

Ranking Donors

Use the suggested questions and research to measure the extent of prospective donors' capacity, commitment, and connection to your organization. The higher a person's capacity to give and the stronger the relationship he or she has to your worthy cause, the higher you will rank that person and the more attention you will want to show him or her. Select a rank of A, B, or C for each donor's capacity to give (with A being the highest and C the lowest). Then grade each donor 1, 2, or 3 based on the strength of that donor's existing relationships to your organization (with 1 being the highest and 3 the lowest).

When you are through assigning letters and numbers, arrange the names of your donors on a grid of the nine categories, A1 to C3 (Figure 8.2). Any person in the A1 rank will be someone with extensive financial resources who gives generously and is also significantly involved in the

---

FIGURE 8.2

The 3C's Grid: Ranking Capacity, Commitment, and Connection.

(vertical axis label) Higher Commitment and Connection →

A1	B1	C1
A2	B2	C2
A3	B3	C3

← Higher Capacity

organization. Any person in the C3 category will be someone with relatively moderate means who currently has low levels of involvement with the organization.

The A list contains potential givers with the greatest financial capability. Your largest outright gifts, though, may be coming from the A1, A2, B1, and C1 categories. A C1 donor may give more than an A2 donor because the C1 donor has a stronger connection to the organization. A1 donors give significantly now and have the capability to continue doing so. People ranked 2 or 3 in any letter category have the potential to give more within their financial ability. How do you move them up the ranks? Increasing their involvement with the organization is the key.

There are controllable and noncontrollable aspects to the rating categories. At any one time, an individual's giving capacity is beyond your control. To a certain extent the same is true of an individual's commitment. An individual could be, for example, a board member, a member of the annual benefit committee, and have a particular giving history. Connection is the variable you can work with. By increasing a person's connection to the organization you can increase his or her motivation to give. Connection is the flexible variable. You can influence it, and that's why it is so important. Through keeping people current on the organization's activities, staging events, inviting people to serve on honorary committees, and using the other cultivation and solicitation techniques discussed in Chapter Ten, you can increase people's interest in and sense of ownership in your organization. Donors with an increasing involvement with an organization strengthen their justification for making larger contributions to it.

And remember, rankings are not static over time; review the A, B, and C ratings before every cultivation activity. A donor's status can move at any time—up or down. One way to review these ratings is to look at computer-generated reports of these top donors' gift histories. Don't limit yourself to reviewing their most recent gifts. Someone who has just given $100 may have sent in $5,000 three months ago. The $100 could have been for some special award the organization was funding. Don't drop a donor down from an A to a B or a 1 to a 2 rating on the basis of one gift.

Now, using the donor lists you compiled earlier and To-Do Exercise 8.3, rank your donors for their capacity, commitment, and connection.

TO-DO EXERCISE 8.3

Applying the 3C's Ranking System

Use or adapt the 3C's ranking system in order to answer the question, Whom should I be spending the most time cultivating? Take one of the constituent lists you put together for your organization, for example, contributors, volunteers, subscribers, members, or program attendees. Select from your list a group of top donors. Recall the example of the nonprofit that found one-third of its donors were responsible for 92 percent of contributions. Similarly use a percentage amount appropriate to your nonprofit to determine the donors you should be looking at more closely.

Make notes on what you know or suspect about each donor's ability to give and to help raise money. Determine the donor's interest in your cause based on giving history and the various relationships the donor may have with that cause. Reflecting on each one's capacity, commitment, and connection to your organization, rank your top donors and prospects.

Chapter 9

Involving Your Board

NO FUNDRAISING PLAN is complete unless it includes your board of directors and the activities that involve them, such as board committee meetings, cultivation events, and giving targets, as well as solicitation calls to prospects. Your board can be the front line of your fundraising offense, yet all too often board members are not as involved as you, or they, might want. Is there some way your plan can supercharge the fundraising efforts of board members? How do you mobilize them to name names and approach donors? How can you motivate them to become major contributors themselves? The key is to learn each board member's strengths and interests and use his or her abilities, matching them with needs of your nonprofit. When you do that the effectiveness of your board will increase across three categories of fundraising leadership: giving, getting, and attracting.

Fundraising Leadership

Every nonprofit organization needs a committed board of directors that exercises *fundraising leadership* in at least three ways:

• Giving. Board members must be at the forefront of the effort to make sure your organization has the money it needs to accomplish its goals. Ideally, every board member cares enough about the nonprofit to support it financially. By making meaningful and substantial contributions, board members not only directly aid the institution, they also set a standard and lead the way for others to follow. Their giving shows commitment. It is a whole lot easier to ask a donor for a major gift when you can refer to a similar one recently given by a devoted board member.

• Getting. Getting is synonymous with fundraising. There are many ways board members can help raise money in addition to their own giving. They can make fundraising calls on donors with you (two-on-one works better than one-on-one), chair a benefit, host a breakfast reception, or arrange cultivation events. They can introduce their peers, business associates, and friends to your organization and broaden your network. Board members who are proud of their association with your group and are advocates for your cause will give credibility to your funding appeals.

• Attracting. Ideally everyone on your board will participate in hands-on fundraising. However, there is a value in having celebrity board members whose presence acts as a lodestone, drawing contributions to your group, even though a celebrity who brings outstanding credibility by lending his or her name may not be available to take on a more active fundraising role. Of course, the best situation is to have prestigious board members who also actively aid your worthy cause, as former president Jimmy Carter and his wife, Rosalyn, do when they donate both sweat equity and prestige to Habitat for Humanity's low-cost housing.

Learning About Your Board Members

People joining your board generally have had some relationship with your institution in the past. To some extent they know you, which is one reason they have agreed to serve. They also identify with your mission. Ideally they are joining the team with a certain amount of experience, knowledge, and trust in your organization; otherwise they shouldn't be doing it. But that experience and trust doesn't mean they are going to automatically tell you the prospective major donors they know or run out and ask their friends and colleagues for money.

How do you get your board members to tell you about themselves? An effective way to begin to gather this information is a board survey. This survey should be designed to give you a confidential biography and current résumé for each member and also each member's current assessment of the nonprofit and its worthy cause. Position the survey on your fundraising plan as a kick-off event for finding out about your board members' interests, who they are, and what circles they travel in. It's also a good idea to ask each board member to supply a photograph with the completed survey. One immediate way to use these photos is to show them to staff so they can recognize board members at meetings, receptions, or other gatherings and treat them properly.

Board members should become familiar with the different aspects of your nonprofit's work so they will feel vested in the organization. One of the reasons to learn board members' interests is so the organization can use those interests by matching board member abilities with its needs. You can go about this in different ways as long as the end result is that you find out what each board member particularly likes about what your group does and why.

Not everyone on your board will have the capacity to be a topnotch fundraiser, but you don't want to leave anyone out of the process. With the guidance given in this chapter, you may be able to awaken any sleepers on your board, helping them to develop skills they didn't realize they had and to discover that they can effectively fundraise with you.

An environmental group that felt its board members didn't want to be involved and that needed to motivate them brought in an outside consultant who designed a board member survey. The survey revealed that the issue wasn't that the board didn't want to be involved—members actually wanted to do more. The trouble was that the nonprofit was not effectively using its board members!

You don't need to pay someone else to design a survey. The one provided in To-Do Exercise 9.1 will do the job. Use it as is, or adapt it to better suit your organization and board. You'll be surprised how effective it can be. Administer it yourself; you'll get to know your board members better as you do so (and you'll save consultant dollars).

Stages in the Board Survey

You can tackle the process of administering and analyzing a board member survey in the following five stages.

Stage 1: Tell the Board

Your first step is to tell the board the organization is gearing up to do a board member survey: for example, "We're asking all board members to fill out a survey to help us operate more effectively." If your organization is new and in the midst of forming a board of directors, you can use the survey as one of the steps in the process. Be direct about its purpose and importance: for example, "This survey will assist us with long-range planning. And it will be a tool to help us effectively and efficiently work with each of you. Once we have tallied the surveys and reviewed the results, we will report back."

Some of the information you will be asking for is private, so put the word "confidential" in a prominent spot on the survey. Even so, most people aren't going to write down everything you're looking for on a sheet of paper. The survey is a starting point. It becomes most useful when you sit down with each board member and discuss his or her responses to it.

Stage 2: Deliver the Survey

Don't hand out the survey at a board meeting; there's too much chance it will be misplaced or lost. Send it to your board members at their preferred mailing addresses. Once they get it, you don't want it to sit collecting dust, so you have to express urgency. In your cover letter, give your board members a deadline; allow them about two weeks to return it. Remind them that the survey will allow the organization to put together a profile of the board. Point out that good planning depends on an organizational evaluation and you want the board's perspective. Include some comments about what will happen next. Also include a stamped, addressed return envelope.

Stage 3: Collect the Surveys and Schedule Follow-Up Meetings

After the surveys have been turned in, promptly set up a one-hour meeting with each board member. Be sure to leave yourself enough time to review the surveys before the meetings. Give yourself the same two weeks to review and tally them as the board had to fill them out. If surveys are not turned in promptly, call board members to ask for them. If some still don't turn up, you may have to make an appointment to fill them out with each board member in person. Helping someone fill out the survey is not ideal because you don't get a chance to prep yourself before getting together with your board member. But you can still turn it into a positive situation by discussing each board member's thoughts and ideas as you get the particulars on his or her background and lifestyle choices.

Stage 4: Review the Surveys

It's your job to analyze the information contained in the surveys.

Skim through them first. If no one has signed up to serve on the development committee or expressed interest in fundraising, then you have a situation that needs remedying pronto. In your meetings with board members you will need to make clear, in the nicest terms possible, that fundraising is part of their board responsibilities.

When you get down to the actual analysis, you will have three major objectives:

1. Understanding board perception: What do board members see as the nonprofit's strengths and weaknesses? What areas need to be improved? Where is program expansion warranted?

2. Understanding board involvement: How do board members see themselves currently serving the nonprofit? How would they like to see themselves serving the nonprofit?

3. Matching interests and needs: What are the links between your board members' interests and the needs of your nonprofit? You want to find ways to serve both at the same time.

As you review the information your board has given you, you can also try to figure out the people they might know who might also be of service to your organization. One of your ultimate fundraising goals is to build a network of supporters. You will have collected information about where your board members went to college, what year they graduated, the clubs they belong to, and other such pertinent information. When you take that information and add to it where they live, what they do socially, and where they work, you are going to find connections with the projects and needs of your nonprofit.

Your analysis should allow you to create hypotheses about people you've been interested in contacting *whom a board member might already know.* You might be interested in raising money from a certain company and see that one of your board members went to the same college as the head of that company. You might find that one of your board members belongs to the same club as one of your major prospects. If a member of your board works in the banking industry, you might ask whether he or she knows the people in financial services whom you have begun to cultivate.

Put a mark next to the survey answers that suggest areas of mutual interest to the organization and the board member. Jot down a note to remind yourself to check the possibilities. As you review, remember, *you're preparing to sit down with each board member and explore how to capitalize on the person's interests to accomplish the goals of your worthy cause.*

Stage 5: Meet with Each Board Member

Now it's time to get together with each board member privately, in a relaxed setting, perhaps over a meal, to talk about the organization's projects and the board member's interests. To help board members understand that they are on the inside team, share information about the organization that is not generally known. For instance, a board member of the American Museum of Natural History interested in scientific research on mammals might be fascinated to learn that the museum has the largest collection of articulated whale skeletons in the world or that the Bronx Zoo regularly gives its animals that have died to the museum and that the museum uses carnivorous beetles to eat their bones clean so their skeletons can be added to the collection and studied.

Here are some specific items to cover when you sit down with each board member:

- Talk about a specific interest the board member has that matches the nonprofit's activities, and invite the person's further participation in it.

- Give the board member a list of names of prospects you have profiled who would make ideal donors to your organization, and discuss whether he or she can help you with them.

- Ask the board member about personal commitment; begin discussing the board member's own contribution.

- Discuss ways to build a constituency for the organization; enlist the board member's cooperation (for example, as the host of a breakfast, lunch, or reception for donors and prospects in the board member's home or office).

Also, when designing the board survey, analyzing the results, and finally meeting with board members, it's helpful to keep in mind the variety of reasons why people choose to serve on the boards of nonprofit organizations. They include, but are not limited to, the following:

- Personal commitment and belief in your cause

- Increased exposure to topics of interest

- Part ownership of the important achievements of your nonprofit

- Enjoyment from meetings with your group

- Exposure to new people for personal and business reasons

- A leadership role on a board committee devoted to the person's specialty

- Career advancement

- Community service

- Broader experience

- Recognition that family members have benefited from the organization's services

During your private meetings with individual board members, do not expect trust in five minutes. This is the beginning of a long-term, ongoing relationship. Strengthening this relationship takes time, and you, other staff, and the board members need to be doing things together, such as board outings, retreats, and so forth, to generate confidence in each other. The end result you want is that every board member becomes involved in the fundraising effort (getting), contributes money personally (giving), and becomes better and more effective at promoting your institution (attracting).

Now you can begin work on your own survey by completing To-Do Exercise 9.1.

Putting the Survey on the Fundraising Plan

In order to create your fundraising activities schedules and calendar (Chapter Twelve), you will need to know how long each of the five stages in the board survey should take.

Say your next board meeting is September 1. Anchor your survey on that date. That's when you'll introduce it to the board members.

Promptly after the meeting, send the surveys to board members' preferred mailing addresses with the brief, explanatory cover note.

Schedule two to three weeks to receive the completed survey, the amount of time you set as a deadline. If you haven't gotten them back by then, call and ask for them. Allow one or two weeks for collecting laggard surveys, but schedule this collection period concurrent with the next stage.

Then schedule the individual meetings and review the individual surveys in preparation. Allow another two weeks for your review and four weeks for the meetings (that is, about three or four meetings per week, depending on the size of the board).

If you can get relatively prompt meetings with board members, then the whole process will take between five or six weeks. What if a board member just doesn't buy into the process? Well, as we discuss later, that may tell you something too. The board survey is a useful tool for starting a dialogue with board members who have temporarily lost interest in an organization or should retire from their position on the board.

Take a few minutes now to determine your survey schedule by completing To-Do Exercise 9.2.

When to Use the Survey

If you're starting from ground zero, and you want to develop an effective fundraising operation, administer the survey to everyone on the board.

TO-DO EXERCISE 9.1

Preparing the Board Survey

Modify the board survey that follows to suit your nonprofit. Include questions relevant to your fundraising effort.

Should you do this exercise if you already have an involved, committed board of directors? Yes! Even if you have an enthusiastic board of directors, it is essential to regularly get a fresh update on members' views and how their interests match your projects.

[Worthy Cause]
Confidential Board of Directors Survey

Date _____

NAME: Year you joined the board:

• HOME ADDRESS: PHONE:

COMPANY NAME: TITLE:

Name of secretary or assistant: Phone:

• WORK ADDRESS: PHONE:

Please check the address where you would prefer to receive board mailings.

NAME OF SPOUSE:

EDUCATION (colleges attended and degrees received):

_____

Memberships in associations, social clubs, service clubs, and so forth:

Other volunteer activities:

TO-DO EXERCISE 9.1, continued

Special interests and hobbies:

Please give us your answers to the following questions:

1. What was your primary reason for joining the board?

2. What do you think are the most important services that the organization provides?

3. How do you think the organization could better serve its mission?

4. What do you see as the organization's greatest strengths?

5. What are its biggest weaknesses?

6. How would you like to see the organization grow and/or change?

7. In which of the following areas do you have strengths that could be used to help the organization?

_____ Accounting

_____ Artistic

_____ Community affairs

_____ Financial

_____ Fundraising

_____ Investment

_____ Legal

_____ Management

_____ Political

_____ Programming

_____ Public relations

_____ Strategic planning

8. How do you feel that you can best serve this organization?

9. Can you suggest two or three people to be considered as potential board candidates?

Note: Please attach a recent photograph of yourself.

After that, whenever new people join your board, they should complete surveys so you can identify their strengths and weaknesses.

A board survey is not something you need to do every year; that would wear people out. However, board members' circumstances change over time, and the organization changes too. So ask board members to fill out a survey again when the organization expands or when its needs change markedly. One North Dakota fundraiser, for example, used a board survey to reapproach board members for gifts in the wake of the 1997 disastrous spring flood there.

You might also ask board members to complete a survey when a matching grant ends or government funding is cut from a well-loved program or an important board member passes away or another finds she cannot be as active as before. Remember that in today's difficult fundraising environment, raising charitable dollars entails knowing the skills and connections of board members and figuring out new ways to use them creatively. Keep yourself up to date on your board members' profiles.

TO-DO EXERCISE 9.2

Putting the Survey on Your Fundraising Plan

Mark dates on your fundraising plan corresponding to the five stages of the board survey.

Working with the Survey and Interview Information

In the one-on-one interviews, your board members told you how they can help your organization. Before you leave each meeting, decide when you'll follow up on their offers. Say, "I'll get back to you in a week," or, "I'll send you the information you wanted and check with you after you've had a chance to review it." Mark on the fundraising calendar (Chapter Twelve) the action that you've said you would take. Their shows of interest are what you've been after; you don't want to lose these opportunities through failing to follow up! Take notes on a card. Write down everything that your board member has offered to help with or shown an interest in and any next steps you or the board member are going to take with that information. Write down the key prospects board members say they can introduce you to, the cultivation activities they want to host or help organize, and the other contacts or helpful information they have.

Create Board Member Files

In addition to scheduling follow-up steps, create a file for each board member. Keep the person's photo inside. Attach the board interview card to the survey and put it in the folder. Include the names of the prospective donors you discussed and the board member's responses. You will want to track which of these prospects the two of you have contacted for the organization and the status of your gift requests.

Any other board member materials you or other staff come across should also go in these files. For example, one development associate doing some donor research in the library came across an article that mentioned a board member of the charity she was working for. The article described a benefit committee this woman served on and mentioned a number of other prominent wealthy people. The associate put that article in the board member's file, made a note that the woman had the potential to help stage a benefit, and added the names of the members of that benefit committee to a master list of potential prospects to research and discuss with the board member.

Understand What You Need to Do for Your Board

Finally, in addition to educating your board members about your organization and the involvement you expect from them, you and other staff have a responsibility to do the following for them:

- Keep them up to date on the organization's crucial issues, concerns, and financial and fundraising matters.

- Schedule productive meetings that stay within a promised timeframe.

- Keep in regular touch without swamping them with phone calls and mail.

- Don't overburden them with minutia.

- Listen to their ideas.

- Involve them in long-term planning.

- Be profuse with thank-yous and acknowledgments for help given.

Chapter 10

Planning Your Cultivation and Solicitation Activities

AFTER TARGETING the individuals most likely to support your organization, you want to take steps to generate a list of cultivation and solicitation activities for your master plan. You want to develop relationships with prospective donors to the point where asking for and receiving a contribution is a natural result. There are many effective ways to cultivate prospective donors, whether in person, by telephone, or by letter. These days even the fax machine and e-mail can be appropriate tools.

Specific fundraising activities vary widely, from benefits and auctions to incentive giving, membership, and subscription drives. Which ones are best suited for your nonprofit? In general, any fundraising tactic will work best with people who have a strong relationship with the nonprofit and become less effective the more tenuous the connection. However, for greatest success the cultivation and solicitation techniques you select must match the donors you are trying to reach.

Although the fundraising techniques explored in this chapter are not meant to be exhaustive, they do present the important aspects of the principal ways nonprofits cultivate and solicit donors. As you go through them, frequently ask yourself which would be the more effective for your natural donor base.

There are six principal ways most nonprofits actually cultivate donors and ask for money:

- Face-to-face requests
- Fundraising events and benefits
- Personalized letters
- Telephone appeals

- Scheduled mailings to in-house lists
- Direct-mail "Dear Friend" letters

In Chapter Nine you evaluated your prospective donors according to their capacity, commitment, and connection. Now you will use those 3C's rankings to help you decide which fundraising activities are best suited for your prospects. There are no hard and fast rules, but the following fundraising activities are generally most effective with the prospective donors ranked opposite them.

Fundraising Activity	Prospective Donors
Face-to-face requests	A1–A3, B1–B2, C1
Events and benefits	All grid donors, A1–C3
Personalized letters	All grid donors, A1–C3; different levels receive different personalization
Telephone appeals	B3, C2–C3
Scheduled mailings	B3, C2–C3, off-grid prospects
Direct-mail "Dear Friend" letters	Off-grid prospects

Face-to-Face Requests

By far the most effective way to generate large gifts is to talk to donors in person. Studies support what fundraisers know from experience—the closer the relationship between the person asking for the gift and the prospect, the greater the chance that a contribution will be made and the larger the contribution is likely to be. Face-to-face fundraising is particularly effective and appropriate with A1–A3, B1–B2, and C1 donors. They have capacity, commitment, and connection profiles that make it worth the time that personalized fundraising takes.

Having said that, we also point out that it is worthwhile to invest time cultivating B3 and C2–C3 relationships when an exceptionally strong linkage exists between a prospect and your organization. If a board member, for example, knows a C3 prospect well, then plan a cultivation strategy for that prospect. Personal solicitation is your best chance to move this person up the grid.

What if your organization is traditionally funded through lots of smaller contributions rather than a relatively small percentage of larger contributions? Or through some combination of donors and gifts that is between these extremes? Two nonprofits might raise the same total dollars from donor groups with entirely different profiles. One might raise 90 percent of its contributions from fifty people, whereas a second might have to receive five hundred gifts to reach the same amount. For the latter nonprofit, personalized solicitation may simply be too costly.

Cultivating Major Donor Prospects

From your research you have identified your top individual prospects. As we have said, personalized cultivation and solicitation is the preferred method with these individuals, so your goal is to meet and get to know each of them, and you must look for introductions. By the time you meet with your prospects, you should have a pretty clear idea of what might attract them to your institution. And that's the fun part, starting a conversation with your prospect about an area he is interested in. Build on this relationship over time, to the point where the prospect's interest naturally expresses itself. When you do that, as the following example shows, a gift is not far behind.

There is a wonderful woman who was a prospect for an orchestra because she was on the benefit committee of a similar organization. The executive director of the orchestra hadn't met her, but knew that she was a serious music lover. The problem was that she already had a large number of commitments. How could he get her interested in his project? Then he found they had a friend in common, a person who had been on an overseas golfing trip with her. He got the friend's permission to use his name. So when he called and asked if he could get together with her for tea, she didn't turn him down. She felt some sense of obligation. That was one step toward turning her into a donor.

What was needed next, as is often the case, was a more personal connection to the cause to get this philanthropist more interested. The executive director found out that she had provided money through a nearby orchestra for a young European violist who had also played with the director's orchestra. That young musician turned out to be an important link. She had helped pay his living costs, but she had never been introduced to him.

The executive director arranged a meeting between the young musician and his patron. It turned out to mean a great deal to her. And she became a donor to the orchestra. As can often occur in fundraising, the lives of all the people involved were enriched by the experience.

Cultivating Board Members

As we discussed in Chapter Nine, your board members are a special group of top prospects. Every board member should support your organization financially, even if it is a token amount, and that goes for figureheads on your board, too. When board members make personal contributions to a nonprofit, they become more vested in it, they have a personal stake in it, *and you want your board members to feel like large stakeholders.*

Board giving communicates a special commitment to people outside your nonprofit. When board members solicit prospects, you want them to be able to say that the board is 100 percent behind your organization.

Ideally, the board chair or the head of the board development committee will ask other board members to give, otherwise you or someone else from the development area will have to ask them. Each board member should be asked *individually.* And always try to ask for a specific amount. Review board members' individual files to figure out their giving abilities. If someone on your board has limited resources, acknowledge that by suggesting an amount relative to her ability. For the people who haven't been giving anything or who are giving minimally, set a standard gift that everyone on the board should shoot for. It's beneficial to have some minimum level of giving, even if it's only $100. However, always talk individually about their gifts to board members who are large donors.

Soliciting Other Kinds of Help

We know a college president who was introduced to a wealthy philanthropist by one of his trustees, a college alumnus. The philanthropist became an important contributor to the college. The alumnus who introduced the philanthropist has made gifts to his alma mater, but his personal resources are limited. With the introduction, he found another way to make a major contribution to his school.

Getting board members and other contributors to become involved in the solicitation process gives them another way to support your organization. Donors with corporate contacts or whose personal or professional lives relate to your work can make introductions for your organization, and they can become volunteer fundraisers or solicitors.

It will typically take some work on your part to get volunteer solicitors involved, and their concerns have a long history. In his autobiography, Ben Franklin tells us how he too was concerned with the possibility of oversoliciting his friends.

It was about this time that another Projector, the Revd. Gilbert Tennent came to me, with a Request that I would assist him in procuring a Subscription for erecting a new Meeting-house. . . . Unwilling to make myself disagreeable to my fellow Citizens, by too frequently soliciting their Contributions, I absolutely refus'd. He then desir'd I would furnish him with a List of the Names of Persons I knew by Experience to be generous and public-spirited. I thought it would be unbecoming of me, after their kind Compliance with my Solicitations, to mark them out to be worried by [others], and therefore refus'd also to give such a List. He then desir'd I would at least give him my Advice. That I will readily do, said I; and, in the first Place, I advise you to apply to all those whom you know will give something; next to those whom you are uncertain whether they will give any thing or not; and show them the List of those who have given; and lastly, do not neglect those who you are sure will give nothing; for in some of them you may be mistaken.

He laugh'd, thank'd me, and said he would take my Advice. He did so, for he ask'd of every body; and he obtain'd a much larger Sum than he expected, with which he erected the capacious and very elegant Meeting-house that stands on Arch Street [Franklin, 1964, p. 201.

It's normal for people to be reluctant to tell you right off whom they know who might want and be able to assist the organization. The tip we suggested earlier for board members will work with other committed supporters too: show them a list of prospects you hope to solicit *whom you think they might know.* Once people become truly committed to your organization and have successfully raised money for it, they will become more like go-getters on their own initiative. But while you're building this relationship, you have to prove that you are on the ball in researching prospects and methods. And one way to do this is to initiate prospect contact ideas. Once a level of trust and involvement has been established, your volunteer solicitors will become more active. But it will take time.

Training Volunteer Solicitors

Some board members and other volunteer solicitors may want to contact only people they don't know, refusing to solicit their friends. In general, however, don't expect board members and others to contact prospects they don't know well. And when there is a positive connection, a volunteer solicitor's involvement can be the key to a successful solicitation.

Back in Chapter Nine we spoke about the need to train people on your board who are ready and willing to help you solicit major prospects. Here

Getting Help from Your Board Member's Secretary

Your nonprofit's board members can be instrumental in introducing your worthy cause to foundations and corporations. With their busy schedules, however, much of your communication with them may be handled by their support staff. That makes these assistants an important part of the process. Wealthy individuals often have secretaries or assistants too. Be sure to make board members', donors', and volunteer solicitors' staff feel they are appreciated. You want them to care about your organization too. Sending holiday cards and occasional perks from your organization is a nice gesture. If they care about your organization, they are going to keep it on their employer's front plate.

is how you and your volunteer (a board member or some other committed supporter) can work together to raise money for your worthy cause.

Schedule the Meeting

Arrange the times when your board member can go on a solicitation call with you. Ideally, the board member or his secretary will then call the prospect you've identified to schedule a visit. Another approach is to draft an introductory letter about the nonprofit for your board member to send to the prospect. It might say, in part, "I am on the board of this organization. I deeply believe in their work and think it might interest you because [list the reasons]. The enclosed information packet will give you a brief overview of this worthy cause. I'll call you in a few days to arrange a time when we can get together to talk about this cause in greater detail." Then either the board member follows up with the prospect in a few days or you call or the secretary calls to set a date. Your job at this point is to facilitate the appointment process so that you and your board member can go together to meet with the prospective donor.

Hold the Meeting

Here are four most important things to do when asking a prospect for money:

- Know what projects need funding: you should be able to describe in some detail the programs you're going to ask support for.

- Have a clear idea of the amount you want so you can ask for a specific sum, or offer a choice from a smorgasbord of three projects or three aspects of one project with different price tags, all within a range appropriate to the donor. If that doesn't work, have a fallback position: offer the option of contributing to a project without committing a fixed sum.

- Be a good listener: remember, one of your top goals in addition to communicating about your worthy cause is to learn more about your prospect. You're not a one-person band! Give the person you're meeting with time to tell you about his or her own interests.

- If you don't have the answer to a question, say so: remember, it's best to be straightforward. Say that you'll get back with a response as soon as possible.

Leave a Pleasant Reminder

Leave some reference materials with your prospect, choosing those that best represent your organization—*not* your audit or your 501(c)(3) letter but a sampling of materials from your press kit reflecting the character of your organization. If you have an informative annual report, you might choose that, or you might select a newsletter describing your organization's recent activities and a magazine article praising the institution.

Follow Up

After the meeting prepare a follow-up letter from you and the board member to your prospect. It should reflect what you have learned about the prospect's interests in your organization and make a specific written request for a contribution or confirm the gift agreed on at the meeting.

A week or two later call the prospect about the status of your request. One possible opening is to inquire whether the prospect has any questions about your proposal or would like any additional material about your program.

The prospect might give you a yes and a commitment right then. If not, try to keep the conversation moving in a positive direction. Even if you get a no, try to get more information about the prospect's interests so you will know how to come back in with a request that will get a yes.

Understand When a No Is Not a No

In our experience a prospect's initial no is not always final. It often means "no for now" or "no to this specific request." It's very important to stay positive when a prospective donor is turning down a funding request and not to take it personally or as a permanent rejection.

Don't Overload Board Members with Asks

Each volunteer fundraiser for your organization will have the time, energy, ability, and interest to make a certain number of personal solicitations, or *asks*, on behalf of your worthy cause. In our experience, a general rule is three to five in-person calls a year. The acceptable number will vary from volunteer to volunteer. You might be able to ask specific board members to personally solicit more than three people but don't overload them.

Keep Volunteer Fundraisers in the Loop

As you follow up on your cultivation efforts, send copies of letters, faxes, and so forth to the board member or volunteer who came with you to talk to the prospect. It's also important to keep everyone on your fundraising team informed, so staff and other volunteers who might come into contact with the prospect know the stage of the discussions. And it's important to appreciate and acknowledge the help you have received. Make sure to tell the rest of the board about helpful solicitors' good works. Everyone appreciates a well-deserved pat on the back. And it makes volunteers more receptive to helping again the next time they are asked.

Introduce the Personal Element

One of the most effective ways to get people interested in your institution, no matter what donor category they are in, is to give them a first-hand view of what you are doing and the people involved. If you can't bring prospects to your place of operation, as much as possible package up your organization and bring it to them. Introduce major prospects to one of your organization's curators, social workers, or educators. Give them a personal connection to your organization. Remember what great painters like Rembrandt knew, that a violent sea becomes ten times more interesting when you put a small boat with a man, woman, and child in the picture.

How is it that Leon Botstein, president of Bard College, has attracted so many prominent donors? He is adept at satisfying desires in generous people that enhance his own vision for the College. Take Leon Levy, for example, a successful investor who wanted to do something to honor his father, who had been an economist. Bard College owned a Hudson River estate at one end of its campus, once grand but now falling into disrepair. Levy restored this magnificent building, called Blithewood, and set up an economics institute in memory of his father. The building and its grounds are now a jewel on the college campus. The Levy Economics Institute offers an independent program and also adds another dimension to the scholarly work going on at the college.

Or take Susan Weber Soros. Botstein learned that she was interested in running a graduate program in her field of expertise, decorative arts. Together they started a graduate program in New York City that is an adjunct to Bard's undergraduate program. Soros bought a building to house the school, which has developed an extremely prestigious and important program.

Or, finally, take Marieluise Hessel, who had assembled an important contemporary art collection. Botstein found that she wanted to do more than just store it for her own benefit. The result? Ms. Hessel built a facility at Bard, donated her collection to the school, and started a graduate program in curatorial arts, the first in the country.

Further Reading on Major Donors

Zimmerman, R. M. *The Key to Successful Fundraising*. San Francisco: Zimmerman Lehman, 1998.

Fundraising Events and Benefits

Fundraising events can take all sorts of forms: breakfasts, luncheons, or dinners with an honoree; auctions; family functions; cocktail receptions; theater shows; and more. The most social event is an evening benefit party. High-ticket benefits usually include dinner. The possibilities are endless. We once participated in a benefit held at the community-based sports and youth facility Asphalt Green. It was intended for families and took place in the late afternoon. Strawberries and champagne were served and jugglers and stilt walkers performed. The Mayor of New York welcomed guests and endorsed Asphalt Green's project to build an Olympic-

Be Prepared: Genies and Fairy Godmothers Come in Many Different Packages

If somebody comes to your organization and wants to talk about making a gift and you don't know anything about the person, the wisest thing to do is meet with the person and treat him or her with great courtesy. Once a development associate at the Kaufman Cultural Center got a telephone call from a little old lady from Staten Island who said she'd like to visit the center. She was interested in getting involved and wanted to talk about a gift. No one at the center knew anything about her. She asked for subway directions once she got off the Staten Island Ferry. The associate couldn't get anyone else to be there when she met her because no one had ever heard of her, this retired librarian from Staten Island.

It turned out that she had a legacy from a relative and she wanted to give it to a place that dealt with children and music. Years ago she had enjoyed a children's performance at the Kaufman Cultural Center, and that is why she stopped by. And she started giving. Her gifts, which began with a $35,000 donation, were much appreciated, and as she wished, she was kept apprised of projects she could help with. When she died, she remembered the center in her will. She turned out to be a substantial donor.

sized swimming pool. Tickets were reasonably priced because the event was as much a friend-raiser as a fundraiser. Similarly, you should construct your benefit so that it makes sense for your nonprofit and your audience.

Benefit events can be highly productive. When people purchase tickets, they become supporters of your organization. You can put on these cultivation functions at your organization, the home of a board member, or some other friendly setting. Invite people who are on your donor and prospect lists, or form a benefit committee that will ask people involved with the organization (from supporters to suppliers) to come to the event and to invite their friends. At some events it will be appropriate for a speaker to tell the audience about your organization, give a slide presentation, or show a video on your activities.

Awards Events

Nonprofits often honor people who have performed a great service for organizations such as theirs. This kind of event is a good way to reach a wide range of donor and prospect groups, including employees and vendors as well as major supporters. The honored guest could be the president of a local bank, a philanthropist, a board member, or a celebrity who believes in causes such as yours. Ideally, the honoree will be a well-known individual with a number of personal and professional contacts who can work on the benefit committee or be added to the guest list. In addition to selecting an honoree, you will need to find a chairperson who will head-up the benefit committee that raises money and sells tickets for the event.

Although organizing the event usually starts with finding the right person to honor rather than finding the chairperson, it can work the other way too. The person who is chairing the dinner may be the one in a position to invite the person to be honored. Conversely, if you have connections to the person you want to honor and invite him or her yourself, the honoree can often help you identify the right person to chair the dinner. The chairperson should be someone with a close personal or professional relationship with the honoree, someone with a fair amount of clout, who can help draw in other people to participate and come to the event.

In forming the committee, look for people whom the chairperson or honoree have relationships with: their friends and their political, business, and personal contacts. You want to have a benefit committee of at least eight people. Ideally, each member of the committee will buy a table for the dinner or, at a minimum, two tickets. Each committee member is responsible for producing a list of people that she will invite to purchase tickets to the event. In the same way that you develop giving estimates and fundraising activity schedules (see Chapters Eight and Twelve), you develop a benefit committee and ticket buyers. You work through a relationship tree to sell tickets to the event.

We recommend that you have an honoree for your benefit. Benefits function best when they broaden the base of people who will support your organization. The person you honor may have a direct relationship with you, but he or she will also have a whole network of friends and business associates that will be introduced to your organization through this benefit.

Industry-Driven Events

Several New Orleans cultural institutions have identified an effective way to raise money from the real estate community through an industry award benefit honoring a member of that community. A few buddies of the honoree chair the event, just about everyone in the business buys tickets, and most of them show up! People want to see their friends and associates honored. That goes double for a close-knit community like New Orleans's real estate industry.

Certain industries lend themselves better than others to this kind of event. Some have more interconnected commercial relationships than others. If your organization has contacts in the real estate business, this type of award event could be an effective fundraising method. The real estate industry lends itself well to these events because many people are likely to be connected to the honoree: builders, developers, and construction firms and all the people who service the field, such as bankers, insurance agents, and brokers. The auto industry is another example of a business

Recognizing Donors at All Levels

Whether they are giving $50 or $50,000, most people like being recognized for their philanthropy. Donors' names can be put on chair backs, carved into walls, or listed in annual reports. Donors can be given plaques and other awards. Err on the side of generous recognition. Awards and inscriptions can lend a touch of permanence to your donor relationships.

Naming opportunities are endless. Even when people aren't looking for personal recognition, they will often enjoy honoring a family member by dedicating a gift in that person's name. When the Namgyal Monastery in Ithaca, New York, was raising money for the Dalai Lama's podium, donors were offered the chance to have their names inscribed on a plaque attached to that podium. People clamored to be acknowledged as public supporters by this great man and spiritual leader. Of course you will have some people who want their gifts to remain anonymous, but how often do you see donor lists consisting solely of gifts made by "Anonymous"?

with many commercial relationships. In any industry characterized by multiple suppliers who have business relations with a manufacturer, a top executive can count on his or her benefit invitations being accepted.

Friend-Raisers

A *friend-raiser* is an occasion on which your goal is to broaden the base of people interested in your worthy cause. You are trying to expand the number of people you can eventually appeal to for support. Luncheon events, for example, are often used as friend-raisers, or contact-raisers.

When you are trying to expand your business prospect base, breakfast events often make sense. We haven't heard of any held as fundraisers rather than friend-raisers (although that doesn't mean yours can't be the first!). If you are interested in attracting support from the business community and you feel you have a strong case that will appeal to businesspeople, then ask someone from that community who already supports your organization to host a breakfast meeting at his or her office. Schedule it from 8:00 to 9:00 or 8:30 to 9:30 A.M. Invite a group of top corporate executives or corporate contributions officers whose offices are located in the same vicinity, so they can meet briefly to hear your presentation and then get back to work. Make a group appeal for support at the event. Ask attendees individually for their support when you follow-up after they attend the presentation.

Further Reading on Fundraising Events and Benefits

Freedman, H. A., and Feldman, K. *The Business of Special Events: Fundraising Strategies for Changing Times.* Sarasota, Fla.: Pineapple Press, 1998.

Personalized Letters

Letters to donors can be personalized in different ways, according to the recipient. Each letter need to reflect your organization's case statement. (Refer to Chapter Five and the core communications piece you developed for content reminders and ideas on structure.) Just as top donors get invited to a schedule of events, many of which they can attend free in recognition of their generous support, they also always receive personal letters tailored toward their interests. They never get a letter that begins "Dear Friend." They also usually receive personal letters in advance of your meetings with them, briefing them on your organization's activities. This by the way is one time when it is appropriate to fax correspondence. The fax cuts lag time enormously because you don't have to wait until the prospect gets the letter in the mail. Fax it off, and call later that same day or the next to set up the appointment.

People you rate B2–B3 and C2–C3 have the potential to give more than they do now. They get somewhat personalized letters but not as tailored as those sent to the top donors. Their letters will probably begin with a personal salutation—"Dear Ms. Smith"; "Dear Jim"—but basically these are form letters, unless you know a donor is interested in a specific project. In that case the donor receives a more personalized letter on that project. But in regular correspondence from you, this group won't get, "It was so nice to see you," handwritten in the margin, or a P.S. asking, "How are Marty and the kids?" This group also doesn't generally get invited to the president's home for dinner but be sure to invite them to some special events because they probably have the potential to give more than they do now. Lower-level donors get regular mailings. They won't get personalized letters or invitations to those special events unless their gifts increase.

Telephone Appeals

Soliciting a gift by telephone is a big step back from in-person solicitation. The person you're speaking with cannot see you to get an impression of what you are like. She doesn't have a chance to gauge your credibility in person. And you don't have a chance to see her facial expression to assess how she is reacting to your appeal. You don't get to see the environment the person works or lives in or what her taste is. Whereas when you meet with prospects in person, you will often notice telling details about lifestyle and interests, such as award plaques from institutions that have recognized your prospect for doing things that you may not have known she was interested or involved in.

When calling to arrange a meeting, be prepared to succinctly describe what your group does. There's a chance that your prospect won't be willing to set a meeting but will give you some time on the phone to introduce your worthy cause. Try to have a dialogue with your prospect. Talk about what you're doing, why you thought she might be interested in it, and what she could do to help. Listen carefully to the prospect's response and proceed to build your case from there.

Phonathons

One telephone solicitation technique that can be very effective is the phonathon. What nonprofits can benefit? Any that have a sizeable donor, member, volunteer, subscriber, or alumni base. A phonathon can reach a large number of prospects and make targeting small and medium-sized gifts worthwhile. Nonprofit radio stations and public television run these campaigns frequently. And schools raise money from their alumni this way, as do cultural institutions with membership and subscriber lists.

Here's a recipe for running a successful phonathon:

1. Get a group of enthusiastic volunteers to help you make the phone calls. If you're raising funds for a college, get students and alumni to help you. Trained employees will also do.

2. Draft a script of what you would like your callers to say. Having a script is very, very important. Hand it out in advance so your helpers can read it over a few times. They don't have to follow it verbatim, but it will help them communicate the message you want prospects to hear.

3. Set dollar goals. Review a list of everyone you plan to call, and set giving goals. Print out cards showing each prospect's most recent gift as well as his or her largest gift. Set dollar goals for donors at least 25 percent higher than their previous gifts. That way, when people are phoning they have a minimum goal to request.

4. Train your helpers in what to say on the phone and how to react to various responses from the people they are calling. Gather them together a couple of days in advance of the phonathon for a training session in which they form teams to role-play callers and prospects, giving various responses to each other. You will be a floater, available to assist with questions and concerns and to explain what to do when helpers run into a difficult situation. For example, if a prospect has an objection to the program the fundraising is for, the best advice for callers is don't argue. Callers should apologize and say that they will have the development director speak to the prospect. If the prospect doesn't want to be solicited by phone, callers should say they are sorry and that it won't happen again. There must be a space for remarks on the phonathon cards (described in item 6), so callers can note that a prospect does not want to receive telephone solicitations.

5. Most important—have fun! (see the next section).

6. Have phonathon cards ready with information about the people being called and pledge cards for each caller to fill out. Callers should verify the address of the person they're speaking with on the phone. They should ask if prospects have been receiving information from the organization and if they have any questions about the organization's activities? Callers must write down their notes on the space provided. If the person they are calling is not home, they note that in the remarks section of the

card, along with the time and date they called. If the person asks to be called at another time, they write that down along with when the person would like to be called back. If the person called would prefer to receive a written request for funding, they write that down. At the end of the evening, you will collect the cards for follow-up.

7. After the phonathon, immediately send out pledge cards to those who have agreed to make gifts. Be sure to include a return envelope. Keep a record of the pledges that were made, in case some of them are not fulfilled on time and need follow-up.

Have fun with phonathons. For instance, it's nice to give incentives to your phonathon helpers. The first person to raise $1,000 might get a coupon to dinner for two at a local restaurant, for example. And after the group has raised some stated goal, like $5,000, order pizza for everyone. There are lots of little presents and awards you can give people when they've reached certain dollar marks—tickets to a local movie house, discount coupons at a department store, and so on. Local businesses are usually very open to donating such items ahead of time (including the pizza!).

Incentive Giving

Consider offering incentives to your phonathon donors. Have you ever contributed to your public radio station and received a tote bag or some other gift in return? A friend of ours was raising money from individuals for her college and found that same technique highly successful. People loved getting these gifts, which featured the college's name or mascot. Donors at the first contribution level got a paperweight; the next contribution level up merited a college pin. The incentives worked their way up to a pair of champagne glasses etched with the college name.

Some people feel focusing on incentives detracts from the real reasons people should be giving. Still, incentives can be very effective. Drives featuring incentive giving are similar to membership drives—in fact the two are often coupled—because donors get something in return for their gifts. A donor contributes a certain amount of money and gets in return a magazine subscription, free admission, or an invitation to a special program. (Note that IRS rules require that the value of "goods received" be subtracted from the gift amount when calculating gift deductibility.)

Our friend told us that the incentive giving at her college worked particularly well with middle-range B list donors. Think how public radio and television stations put their names on everything they give you. People love it. The monogram on that tote bag you carry shows that you have made a commitment to the organization and that you're giving to a worthy cause. You're giving something, and you're getting something. And what you're getting demonstrates that you're a giver—and ties you closer to the organization.

That's a nice extra with incentive gifts; they encourage further donations. The gift imprinted with the nonprofit's monogram or mission is a touchstone that continues to remind the donor of the worthy cause. In a quiet, seductive way, it cultivates the donor for the next contribution.

Further Reading on Telephone Appeal and Phonathon Scripts

Warwick, M., and others. *999 Tips, Trends, and Guidelines for Successful Direct Mail and Telephone Fundraising.* Berkeley, Calif.: Strathmoor Press, 1995.

Scheduled Mailings to In-House Lists

One of your goals for mailings to your in-house lists of donors, prospects, and suspects is to make sure that your organization is staying at the forefront of people's thinking. Write to your donors at least three times a year, possibly four. Your best prospect for a gift is someone who's just given to you, and many people give more than once a year. Some will want to contribute two or three times a year. It's important to stay in contact with your donors, update them on what's new at the organization, and let them know how much you appreciate their support. At the same time, you don't want to overwhelm them to the point that they toss out your letters the moment they see the return address.

You don't have to ask for a specific gift each time but always enclose a reply device (see Exhibit 10.1), which might include a return envelope with "Thank you for supporting us" on the inside flap and boxes to check for suggested gift amounts. Provide spaces where donors can write down the names of people they suggest adding to your mailing list.

Schedule of Mailings

Here are some suggested dates to put on your schedule of mailings.

• Donors' giving anniversaries. If someone gives to your organization in April, you want to be sure that donor gets a funding request by January, asking him to repeat and, if possible, increase the support. Be sure to remind the donors how grateful you were when they gave last year, and refer to the amount of their gift.

EXHIBIT 10.1

World Monuments Fund's Reply Device.

Dear World Monuments Fund:

I want to help the Jewish Heritage Program continue its work of identifying and preserving endangered Jewish Monuments. Enclosed is my contribution in support of WMF's Jewish Heritage Program in the amount of:

__	$5,000	Patron	__	$250	Member
__	$2,500	Benefactor	__	$100	Friend
__	$1,000	Sponsor	__	$____	General support
__	$500	Contributing member			

NAME _____

ADDRESS _____

CITY, STATE, ZIP CODE _____

PHONE _____

Please make checks payable to World Monuments Fund: Jewish Heritage Program

A copy of the World Monuments Fund's latest annual report may be obtained from the Office of Charities Registration, Secretary of State, 162 Washington Avenue, Albany, NY 12231

Source: © *World Monuments Fund, 1999. Reprinted by permission.*

- Year's end. So many people give at the end of the calendar year that you want to be sure to send out a year-end mailing between late September and early November to all your donors (except for ones that have just given).

- Early spring. Even if you've done a year-end mailing, you may decide to do another in the early spring. This can be an information piece, like a newsletter, but remember to include a pledge card and an envelope or an envelope with a gift table on the inside flap.

- Pre-summer. Do a mailing by April or early May, before summer sets in (and people go on vacations).

Further Reading on Mailings to In-House Lists

Warwick, M. *Revolution in the Mailbox: How Direct Mail Fundraising Is Changing the Face of American Society—& How Your Organization Can Benefit.* Berkeley, Calif.: Strathmoor Press, 1990.

Direct-Mail "Dear Friend" Letters

Approaching funders through direct mail is a specialty. Going beyond mailings to one's in-house database and getting into the direct-mail business is simply too expensive for most nonprofits. You need large numbers of people whom you're dealing with or whom you think would contribute to your cause to make direct mail worth considering. If you have a national or international cause, or work for a nonprofit with a multi-million-dollar operating budget, then you may want to look into direct-mail options.

Direct-mail charitable appeals can make a good case study in credibility. Consider how tough it is to land unannounced in the midst of competition (other mail) at the home of your prospect and grab the credibility spotlight. That's the task direct mail is up against. In the credibility wars, direct mail occupies the role of the guerilla warrior. So, as an extra-credit exercise, you might try this: keep your list of press kit items handy as you open an unasked-for appeal. Study the press kit items and the letter that make up the direct-mail piece. Then think about them and rate them. Do you believe what they say? Why or why not?

We toss away most direct-mail appeals without a second thought. For this chapter, however, we stopped ourselves in mid-toss in order to analyze a direct-mail piece in terms of credibility, legitimacy, and worthiness. Here's our case study in direct mail—or, "What Not to Do."

The envelope was plain brown with a clear plastic window revealing the edge of a plastic card. These days one might wonder, "Is this a free telephone calling card?" The envelope had an official-looking return address from Washington, D.C., that sounded as if it were across from the White House. Next to our name and address was the message, "Opening this letter may be the most effective way to stop the [name of an extremist group]." Despite our self-imposed assignment, we almost threw it away. We opened the letter and wondered how they were going to convince us they were a worthy cause. We also wondered if we should be on the lookout for possible fraud. What if some unscrupulous people were sending an appeal for funds that they intended to place straight into their own pockets? Unfortunately, it's a fact of life that this does happen, hence some of the complaints received by the National Charities Information Bureau and other charity watchdog agencies.

The direct-mail piece did several things to appear credible:

It offered a page of quotations from news articles praising the organization. Some of the publications we had heard of, others we hadn't. Some of the statements quoted had been made by an executive of the group sending the letter—they were not arm's-length comments. That diminished the credibility of the other quotations for us.

The letter said that a famous individual from Hollywood had started the group. That was impressive. But then we looked, Did that person write the letter? No. An unknown person had signed it. Was the celebrity still associated with this group? We couldn't tell. There were no board members listed on the letterhead or separately.

Maya Angelou, a former Poet Laureate of the United States, was quoted. That impressed us. Later, though, a friend of ours asked us whether the quotation specifically mentioned the organization. Good point. The quotation was on the topic but did not mention the group by name.

How would we rate this mass marketing appeal? The organization did appear to have some respected people endorsing it. Then again, the letter made us nervous because it didn't include a list of board members or supporters. On reflection, we also realized we didn't have a clear idea of how the organization spent its money. That lit a definite caution light. We had no idea how this organization planned to save us from that extremist group either—and actually the letter had not convinced us that we needed saving. That was enough. We don't know if this group is a legitimate 501(c)(3), but whether it is or not, its letter had not convinced us of the group's worthiness or captured our interest.

In summary, this direct-mail piece had these problems:

- It quoted organizational insiders, not outsiders.

- It used quotations from unknown publications.

- It didn't list board members or supporters.

- It didn't convince us that there was a problem (that we needed to be saved from the extremist group) or that the organization had a viable solution to it.

- It presented no proof of 501(c)(3) status.

Further Reading on Direct-Mail "Dear Friend" Letters

Lautman, K. P., and Goldstein, H. *Dear Friend: Mastering the Art of Direct Mail Fundraising*. Rockville, Md.: Fund Raising Institute, 1991.

In To-Do Exercise 10.1 you can use all the information you have collected about your donors to begin selecting appropriate fundraising activities.

TO-DO EXERCISE 10.1

Generating Cultivation and Solicitation Activities

To generate a list of fundraising activities for your master plan, consider the mix of individual donors, prospects, and suspects you have gathered and their capacity, commitment, and connections to your group. Then select the fundraising techniques most likely to raise money for your worthy cause. Write down which general methods you will use to cultivate and solicit donors. Within those categories, write down which specific fundraising methods you think would be the most effective, and why you think so. Consider what return of services or acknowledgment you might offer donors for their contributions.

Chapter 11

Finding Institutional Donors

INDIVIDUALS MAY FORM the core of your supporters, but institutions definitely merit a place in the constellation of prospective contributors. In 1997, corporations and foundations gave away 21.6 billion dollars worth of grants, split 8.2 billion/13.4 billion, respectively (AFFRC Trust for Philanthropy, 1999, p. 22). Although it can take a substantial amount of time and energy to find the best institutional prospects for your worthy cause and to complete their grant applications, the rewards can be significant. In addition to increasing your funds and the public awareness of your organization, receiving an institutional grant can add credibility to your cause, which is always helpful when soliciting new donors.

You can use the same approach to ranking institutional prospects that you used to rank individual prospects, evaluating their 3Cs. In the case of institutions, however, researching their giving capacity is generally a matter of going to public records, as described later. Grantmaking totals are available as well as, in many cases, average grants and other statistics. Commitment is a measure of the extent to which an institution's giving interests match your organization's activities. Connection is a measure of the history your organization has with the institution and of the potential or existing personal relationships.

This chapter gives a quick, reliable way to identify the best institutional donors for your fundraising plan. We'll show you how to put together a preliminary prospect list and then refine it based on close inspection of an institution's giving procedures and its recent grants to other organizations. There is a great amount of information available on corporate and foundation giving, but if you search efficiently you can minimize the time you spend finding and soliciting corporations and foundations.

Zeroing In on Giving Guidelines

The single most important factor in identifying corporate and foundation supporters is to match your organization's activities with an institution's giving interests.

Most institutional giving programs are staffed with full-time professionals. These programs are, if you will, in the charitable giving *business*. Because of their size and the number of requests they receive, companies and foundations articulate their charitable interests in *giving guidelines*. These guidelines can run from one paragraph to several pages. Unlike your top individual prospects, your best institutional donors have most likely never heard of your worthy cause. That's not a problem, however, because institutions make their giving guidelines available to all interested nonprofits.

Giving guidelines often begin with the giving program's mission statement then proceed to the philanthropic areas the program focuses on and an explanation of how to apply for funding. The Consolidated Edison Company, an electric and gas utility in New York City, runs a corporate contributions program that focuses on giving to "Education, Social Infrastructure, and the Arts." The guidelines further define the program's interest in each area. For example, Exhibit 11.1 presents the program's definition of social infrastructure.

In addition to a company's or foundation's giving program guidelines, there are some other important pieces of information that you want to procure.

- Annual report. The more you know about a company or foundation before you submit your grant application, the better your chances will be of getting funded. In addition to presenting the institution's financial information, the annual report is an invaluable source for discovering how the company or foundation views itself. This publication also lists a host of executives and board members that you can review for possible connections with members of your board of directors. Companies use annual reports to promote not only their business activities but also their corporate philosophy, values, and culture. Usually a corporation's public affairs office sends out its annual reports. You can call and request a copy.

- Giving report. Some companies give away enough money to warrant a separate report that describes their recent grantmaking activities. The report tells you what organizations received money and the specific projects that received funding. Check whether any of the funded projects or grant recipients are similar to your organization and its activities.

EXHIBIT 11.1

Example of a Giving Guideline.

The Con Edison Corporate Contributions Program
Social Infrastructure

Con Edison supports programs that invest in four aspects of our service area's social infrastructure: health and human services, community development, civic concerns and the environment.

Health and Human Services. We concentrate on direct support to local hospitals, child care, health education, public health programs and social services.

Community Development. We contribute to programs designed to strengthen the economic and business vitality of low-income areas. These include skills and employment training programs, business assistance programs and housing/neighborhood development programs.

Civic Concerns. We support organizations that benefit a broad geographic cross-section of our service areas. These include programs that focus on youth, law and justice and public policy.

The Environment. We give consideration to programs and institutions that emphasize conservation, environmental education and preservation.

Source: "The Con Edison Corporate Contributions Program" (brochure). Reprinted by permission.

- Grant application form. This is the application form and procedure required by the institution and may or may not be a part of the giving guidelines package. It lists application deadlines and what attachments are required, such as proof of your nonprofit's 501(c)(3) status.

In addition to calling a company or foundation for its giving guidelines, you can often find these guidelines at the specialized fundraising libraries listed in the Appendix. Some institutional donors have placed their giving guidelines on the Internet, the world's largest billboard. It's in a corporation's or foundation's best interests to let nonprofits know what kinds of programs it likes to support so it isn't flooded with inappropriate funding requests.

The good news in the grantsmanship game is that any nonprofit whose activities match an institution's giving interests *should* apply. These match-ups are the prospects you want on your activities schedule. Remember, as competitive as obtaining foundation grants is, by law these institutions must give away 5 percent of their net assets each year. They want to find qualified charities.

How Institutions Target Their Giving

Because searching for institutional donors is a hunt for giving guidelines that match your mission, it is critically important to know the three ways institutions target their giving. As with spinning slot machine symbols, you want a match on all three.

1. By geography: concentrate on local funders because nearly 80 percent of them have giving guidelines that limit their contributions to a certain region, city, or state. Foundations based in New York City, for example, give away over 90 percent of their grant dollars to nonprofits in that state (Foundation Center, 1994).

2. By subject: most institutions focus their giving in specific areas, such as education, health, or the environment, to leverage results and to advance the interests stated in their charter. Review the giving guidelines of institutions you are interested in. Look at the list of organizations they support and their range of gifts. If organizations on this list are similar to yours, you're onto a hot prospect.

3. By type of support: carefully check the types of support your institutional prospects will consider. This information will be invaluable in helping you frame your grant request. Grants are made for all of the following purposes, but not all funders make all of them. You need to check which ones each institution will consider.

   - General operating support: unrestricted money that can be used to cover any nonprofit expenses

   - Project or program support: restricted money designated to fund a specific activity

   - Capital purchases: funds for building projects, from constructing a new performing stage to buying computer equipment and other durable goods

   - Noncash, in-kind gifts: donations such as equipment or the use of office facilities

Who Makes the Decision

Corporations and foundations are inundated with requests for support, so they all have relatively formal application procedures centering on written proposals. A governing board or a committee appointed by that board uses these proposals to make the giving decisions. In the case of corporate grants, the owner or chief executive can often make gifts directly. Some boards allow selected staff members to make certain grants *at their discretion.*

Further Reading on Researching

Foundation Center. *The Foundation Center's User-Friendly Guide: A Grantseeker's Guide to Resources.* (4th ed.) New York: Author, 1994.

Finding Corporate Prospects

Most of us can name a few major national foundations funded by businesses, such as the Ford and Carnegie Foundations, but we all know most of the companies that have a significant presence in our communities and also multinational companies with brand-name products. By their nature corporations are more visible than foundations, and that can make it easier to discover their giving interests.

Large companies with broad-based customers, such gas and electric utilities, insurance companies, and banks, all have community grants programs. The Con Edison Corporate Contributions Program highlighted earlier is just one of many such programs. Because most philanthropically oriented companies are committed to supporting *local* charities, the fact that a large company is headquartered in or does business in your community gives you a legitimate reason to call and ask for its giving guidelines. This is *not* how librarians recommend doing prospect research, but it can be fast and effective.

Rather than head for the library, make your initial list of corporate prospects by taking stock of local companies with lots of customers in the neighborhood where your nonprofit operates. Consider these categories.

Utilities

The local electric company, telephone company, and gas company all have contributions officers who can supply you with information about their giving programs. As Con Edison states in its giving guidelines, "Strong stable neighborhoods are a key to our business success and to long-term regional prosperity. We are committed to contributing to [charitable] activities that advance those goals." In addition to their regular giving programs, regulated monopolies often have smaller grant programs aimed at helping local charitable groups.

Banks and Insurance Companies

Banks and insurance companies can be good prospects, particularly if they have a significant customer base in your community. As with utility companies, there is an element of enlightened self-interest tied to their corporate giving.

National Companies

Do any national companies (for example Kelloggs, Hertz, or Exxon) have headquarters in your community or nearby? If not, how about a local Coca-Cola bottler or a branch of a prominent national or regional company? From what you've heard or read, whether it's in a theater *Playbill* or in a sports program, what local charities do these companies support?

Businesses That Share Your Interests

Businesses whose activities correspond to your programs make good prospects. For example, if you run an early childhood program, you share an interest with children's clothing manufacturers and with toy companies. Think about how your activities relate to what your corporate prospect does. One of the American Russian Youth Orchestra's biggest tour expenses is airfare. ARYO contacted Delta Air Lines when that company was expanding its routes to Eastern Europe and Russia. The new globalization of business made ARYO's and Delta's interests match up, and ARYO's request was funded with an in-kind gift: free air miles on Delta flights.

Businesses That Benefit from You

What companies profit from your organization's existence? These companies are ideal prospects because they have a connection to your cause.

Suppliers

Who are your vendors? What printing, legal, accounting, and banking services do you use? Don't forget to solicit them; they have a self-interest in your success and are knowledgeable about your organization. Solicit your organization's lawyer, accountant, and everyone else you do business with. At a minimum they have a business interest in your survival, and it could be there's a true believer at one of them waiting to be asked to support your worthy cause.

Other Local Businesses

Do stores, restaurants, and other small businesses in your neighborhood benefit from your patronage or the fact that your organization exists? Is there a particular restaurant that your audience and staff frequent? Solicit nearby stores and other attractions that benefit from your patronage. For a hospital, these businesses might include nearby restaurants, pharmacies, and parking garages. The Brooklyn Academy of Music (BAM) solicits the stores immediately surrounding its facility. Without the audience BAM draws and the staff who work there, many of those businesses would cease to exist.

Further Reading on Corporate Fundraising

Brownrigg, W. G. *Effective Corporate Fundraising.* New York: American Council for the Arts, 1982.

Finding Foundation Prospects

The best foundation prospects for your worthy cause have giving interests that match one or more of your nonprofit's activities. Most foundations do not have high profiles like companies looking for public recognition. So to identify foundations with interests coinciding with your own, you will most likely want to consult directories and other reference materials at a specialized fundraising library. Thanks to such libraries (listed in the Appendix), too little information is no longer the problem. The Foundation Center, for example, maintains information on over 40,000 foundations and over 750,000 recently awarded grants. As we've found out while browsing the Internet for fundraising help, the challenge is to stay focused

---

TO-DO EXERCISE 11.1

Finding Corporate Giving Prospects

Considering at least the following categories, list all the corporate prospects in your area.

- Large companies with broad-based customers, such as gas and electric utilities, insurance companies, and banks that have community grant programs.

- Businesses that benefit from your nonprofit's existence, ranging from the company that printed your last benefit invitation to the restaurant where it was held, from suppliers to neighborhood businesses.

- Local offices of regional and national companies that presently support charities similar to yours (look at annual reports on the Internet and other public contributor lists).

Now check this list against your organization's corporate donor and prospect lists to see what new names you have come up with. Consider creating prospect profiles for the new companies.

on what you're after. You're on a mission. Get the prospect information you want and move on to the cultivation stage.

The Foundation Center Libraries

The Foundation Center is a special resource for nonprofit grant seekers, and we urge you to make use of its comprehensive fundraising collections. There are Foundation Center Libraries in New York City, Washington, D.C., Atlanta, Cleveland, and San Francisco. And there are extensive research materials to be found in close to two hundred cooperating Foundation Center collections at libraries in all fifty states.

Foundation Center librarians can be very helpful in directing your search for funders. In addition the center offers regular introductory sessions on how to use its facilities. They are short and to the point, and we recommend you check them out. (To obtain the schedule of offerings, call the Foundation Center at (800) 424–9836, or access the Foundation Center's home page [www.fdncenter.org].)

To simplify your search, use these three steps when you go prospecting for foundations:

1. Create an initial list of prospects by limiting yourself *geographically*. Look at directories that list grants made to nonprofits in your city or state. Then look under *subject indexes* for foundations that give to projects like yours.

2. Narrow your list by checking detailed giving information on each of your foundation prospects.

3. Fill out a copy of the prospect profile in To-Do Exercise 11.4 for each funder whose priorities closely match your project.

Recent Grant Recipients

Is your organization similar to any listed in a foundation profile's sample grants section? If your program seems to fit a foundation's guidelines perfectly, but the sample grants listed do not confirm that, you can get more detailed information by going to the foundation's tax return. As mentioned earlier, foundations must file IRS Form 990PF annually *and* make copies available to interested parties. Each 990 lists *all* the grants the foundation made that year, complete with the amounts and the names of the recipient organizations. Foundation Center libraries have 990s for an extensive list of foundations.

As you're doing this research, you are likely to run across grant recipients in your field whom you know about. Seeing what they've raised money for can inspire your thoughts on how your organization can approach the same foundation for support.

A 990 form will also give you the names of officers of the foundation, its key employees, and the full board of directors. Scan these data for links between your organization and the foundation. A personal contact is always worth discovering. Having a voice inside a donor organization can ensure that your case will be heard.

Are Some Foundations Better Prospects?

Is there a group of foundations that provides a higher rate of success than others? Dealing with small family foundations can be similar to approaching individuals on your top donor list. Often run by the donors that funded them, such foundations can be more flexible in their funding decisions and less bureaucratic than large foundations with paid personnel. Institutional foundations like the Robert Wood Johnson and Ford Foundations have more rigid giving guidelines and are often harder to gain direct access to.

When you are selecting which foundation to go to first, a family foundation or an institutional foundation (and both have similar application deadlines and interests that match your organization), we suggest going where you have the strongest contacts and closest relationships. It is similar to job hunting, house hunting, and car buying. First, approach the people who know you best. The place where you have a personal contact is the place where you have the greatest likelihood of getting a positive response to your program. In the absence of that personal contact, though, we recommend focusing on the smaller family foundations before the large ones.

National and Regional Grantmaking Organizations

Remember the National Network of Grantmakers Common Grant Application Form in Chapter Five? It's accepted by over fifty foundations. Similar common application forms are accepted in regions across the country (see the listing of regional grantmaking associations in Chapter Five). Even though you'll want to tailor each proposal you write to the specific foundation you have in mind, it is still a time-saver to work with just one application form. So it can be worthwhile to *put the list of foundations and corporations that accept the common application form on your initial prospect list.* Then check the giving interests of each of those foundations. If even a handful of them give to your type of program, you're ahead of the game. You'll be able to efficiently process proposals to them.

Often local groups of foundations hold informational seminars for nonprofits, talking about what foundations do and how they do it. Set up to encourage an exchange of information, these seminars are a chance for nonprofit staff to hear foundation officers at firsthand and to network with other nonprofit professionals. Get in touch with your local grant-makers association, get on the association mailing list, and attend association seminars. Go up to the people at these get-togethers, introduce yourself, give them your card, and briefly describe your organization. Let them get to know you and your organization.

Further Reading on Foundation Fundraising

Foundation Center. *Foundation Fundamentals.* (5th ed.) New York: The Foundation Center, 1994.

Using Personal Contacts

To whom should you present your funding case at a corporation or foundation? If you are fortunate enough to know a decision-maker at your prospective corporate or foundation donor or have some other connection with a funder, this can increase the odds in your favor. If you or one of your board members is on personal terms with a top executive or CEO of a corporation or foundation, make use of that relationship. It won't guarantee you a gift, but it will cut through a lot of layers of bureaucracy, and it is always helpful to have a friendly ear.

Companies where your members or constituents, volunteers, and

---

TO-DO EXERCISE 11.2

Finding Foundation Prospects

Get a copy of the common application form of a regional or national grantmaking organization. Research the giving guidelines of the foundations that accept it. Which foundations have giving interests that match what your organization does? Refine the list accordingly until it lists just the best matches for your nonprofit.

employees' family members work make good prospects. Those people can vouch for your organization's work. After the Brooklyn Skyhawks got their first grant, for example, a coach who worked at a bank was inspired to visit the bank's contributions officer to tell him about the Skyhawks. The bank made a small contribution immediately even though its official application deadline was past. And it invited the Skyhawks to submit a full application for consideration at the bank's next contributions meeting. Once you begin receiving such contributions, be sure to keep the contributions officers informed about your organization's activities. You want all your supporters to feel that they are a part of your team and knowledgeable about it.

What if an institution's giving interests don't match, but you know someone there? As we pointed out earlier, if you know someone on the board or a top executive or someone who thinks he can champion your cause, then you can bend the rule about not putting institutions on your list unless they match your interests. You can explore with your personal contact in more detail what the institution's current interests are, how flexible those interests are, and other routes into the application process. If that discussion doesn't produce encouragement, however, you don't need to spend more time spinning your wheels, because there are enough places out there that *will* have interests that fit yours.

Seeking Corporate Sponsorship

The nature of corporate giving has changed within the last fifteen years, with corporate sponsorship becoming more important and corporate charitable contributions diminishing. A corporation's contributions budget may be relatively small and already overcommitted, but sponsorships come out of different corporate pockets, such as marketing, advertising, and public relations. Corporate sponsorships are endorsements. The company's name is linked with your worthy cause, and you both get visibility. The company expects that an association with your organization will encourage a positive public response, that people will like what the company is doing and as a result buy its product or use its services.

A sponsorship can turn out to be a much more substantial gift than a simple charitable contribution. With a corporate sponsorship you may get not only an out-and-out contribution of $5,000, $10,000, or $50,000 for your project but also help with items that enhance the corporate image. You may get print and radio ads paid for by the corporation and access to corporate services like printing and logo and brochure design.

Understanding What Makes a Corporate Sponsorship Work

No matter what a corporation says about being community minded, most businesses give primarily out of self-interest. Corporations are looking for ways to enhance their public image and for causes that relate to what they're doing. Again, you're a detective when seeking out corporate sponsorships. Once you figure out your answers to the two questions that follow, you might even succeed in marketing yourself to a corporation that has never thought about sponsorship with a nonprofit.

- How does the population you reach match the population your corporate prospect is trying to reach?
- How would aligning with your program benefit that corporation?

Of course you are not going to be answering these questions for lots of corporations. There isn't time. *You're looking for a corporation whose activities clearly fit with what you're doing and where you can get access to a decision-maker.*

Think of an airline company sponsoring the Special Olympics. It can state, "We are the official airline carrier of the Special Olympics." Its name and this image are broadcast around the world. It is able to put out the message that it is an airline that cares about the community. And it has the right to print this information on all its advertising and PR material. Also the Special Olympics will credit the airline as its "official airline" in all of its literature. Similarly, consider the benefits the Saturn Corporation gets from its sponsorship of a program for the Boys & Girls Clubs of America (Exhibit 11.2).

Look at the way a corporation has positioned itself. Look at how it has traditionally supported charitable organizations. Ask yourself how you can fit into its approach. Look for medium-sized corporations that sell consumer products, and profile them. Ask yourself how their support for your organization would benefit their business. When you do this, you are developing a marketing plan for your nonprofit program.

Communicating How Your Nonprofit Can Help the Company

Sponsorship is a rapidly changing area. Corporations have become more sophisticated and now realize that it's in their self-interest to give away their so-called philanthropic monies in ways that spotlight their products. But unless *you* explain the benefits of associating with your nonprofit, the

EXHIBIT 11.2

Saturn Cycle Recycle Program Ad.

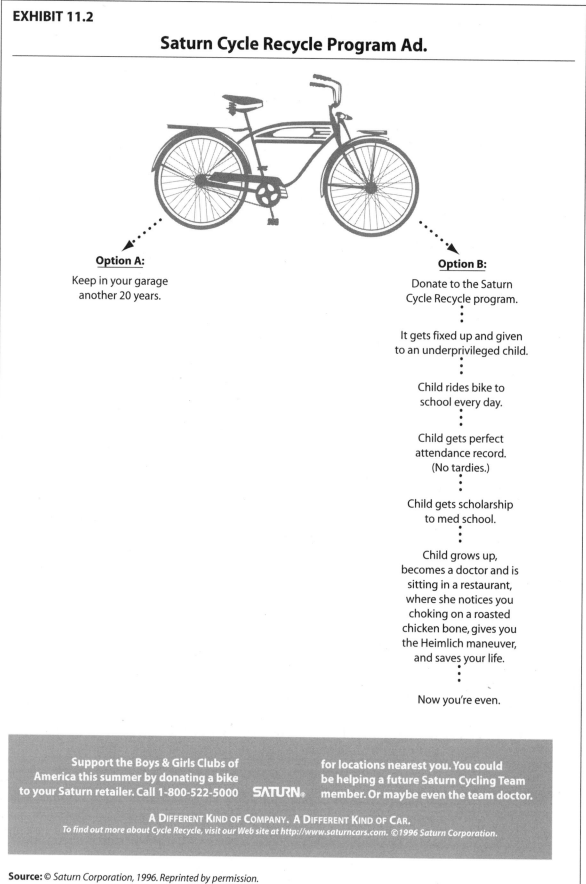

Option A:

Keep in your garage
another 20 years.

Option B:

Donate to the Saturn
Cycle Recycle program.

It gets fixed up and given
to an underprivileged child.

Child rides bike to
school every day.

Child gets perfect
attendance record.
(No tardies.)

Child gets scholarship
to med school.

Child grows up,
becomes a doctor and is
sitting in a restaurant,
where she notices you
choking on a roasted
chicken bone, gives you
the Heimlich maneuver,
and saves your life.

Now you're even.

**Support the Boys & Girls Clubs of
America this summer by donating a bike
to your Saturn retailer. Call 1-800-522-5000** SATURN® **for locations nearest you. You could
be helping a future Saturn Cycling Team
member. Or maybe even the team doctor.**

A DIFFERENT KIND OF COMPANY. A DIFFERENT KIND OF CAR.
To find out more about Cycle Recycle, visit our Web site at http://www.saturncars.com. ©1996 Saturn Corporation.

Source: © *Saturn Corporation, 1996. Reprinted by permission.*

chances are the company won't figure them out. Exhibit 11.3 is a version of a sponsor benefits piece that gives one idea of how to do this.

Approaching a Corporation for Sponsorship

Part of the challenge is locating the right person in the corporation to hear your case for sponsorship. Each corporation's organization chart is different, so talk to the public affairs office first. Find out who is in charge of marketing and who handles special events. Ask who the company's PR agency is. Who its advertising agency is? Generally the corporate giving officer is not the person who handles sponsorships.

If you target smaller and medium-sized companies as opposed to a huge one, there will be fewer decision-makers involved with reviewing your proposal. It may also be useful to market your organization initially on two fronts, to the corporation and to the advertising agency.

Once you find the right person to approach, start sending material that builds credibility for your worthy cause and shows how associating with it can help the corporation. Obviously the best approach is to start at the top. If you know someone who knows the head of the corporation, start there. Work your way down to the right person. If it's a corporation you think you have a real angle for and you can't find anyone who has a top contact there, then start exploring on your own. Talk to a number of different people. Ask each one whom you should be speaking with at the company. Who handles advertising inside the company? Who is the advertising agency? Who is the company's service representative at the agency? Who deals with sponsorships in the advertising agency?

Filling Out a Prospect Worksheet

After you have confirmed that a foundation or corporation has giving interests that match your project, study the grant application procedure listed in the institution's giving guidelines and other materials and then fill out the prospect worksheet in To-Do Exercise 11.4.

Getting Attention for Your Proposal

Your worthy cause will stand a much better chance of getting funded when donors have a clear understanding of its activities and its needs. The challenge is to make your case quickly and clearly. Foundation and corporate contributions officers are inundated with hundreds of requests for money each week; so whether your organization is a concert hall presenting new

EXHIBIT 11.3

Communicating the Benefits of Sponsoring Your Organization.

Worthy Cause

Address: Tel: Fax:

Sponsor Marketing Benefits

Presence Marketing

• Worthy Cause *press conferences* include Sponsor spokespersons.

• Sponsors receive *recognition* in all Worthy Cause media coverage.

• *Signage* prominently includes Sponsors.

• *Print advertisements* link Worthy Cause and its principal Sponsors.

• *Commercial spots* are available for sponsorship.

• *Design wear* with corporate logos worn by Worthy Cause program staff members.

Product Distribution

• Worthy Cause gives out Sponsor's products at all special events.

• Worthy Cause will investigate distribution of Sponsor's products at program sites.

Networking Opportunities

• Top executives and government officials host *special events.*

• Sponsors host *receptions* at special events for major clients.

Employee Benefits

• *Volunteer opportunities* will pair employee and families with Worthy Cause programs in a philanthropic exchange.

• Experts from Worthy Cause will give talks on program expertise to Sponsor employees.

• Worthy Cause will hold a *special program* for employees.

Community Outreach

• *Incentive programs* allow *local youths* to attend Worthy Cause events.

• *Young Peoples Volunteer Program* is under consideration.

• *Special events* are held for community volunteers and community groups.

• *Dinners with executive director and program managers* can be hosted in the homes of corporate executives.

TO-DO EXERCISE 11.3

Finding Corporate Sponsorship Opportunities

Corporations look for causes that enhance their public image and that relate to what they do. Answer the two questions below to come up with two or three corporate sponsorship prospects:

- How does the population you serve match the population the corporation is trying to reach?
  _____
  _____
  _____

- How would aligning with your program benefit the corporation?
  _____
  _____
  _____

Draft a script for a telephone call to your top prospects inquiring about sponsorship opportunities. In a few sentences (the time you would have on the phone), what would you tell them about your organization? How would you proceed to present the benefits of sponsorship?

TO-DO EXERCISE 11.4

Institutional Prospect Profile

Complete the following institutional prospect profile for the foundation or corporation you have selected as a prospect. Modify the profile as needed to fit your nonprofit's requirements.

Institutional Prospect Profile

Funder's name:

Address:

Phone and fax:

Contact person:

Giving Data

Total grants made:

TO-DO EXERCISE 11.4, continued

Range of grants:

Examples of grant recipients *like our organization* and amounts given:

Giving Interests
Geographic limitation:

Subjects that match our project (include populations served):

How well does this match what our organization does? High, medium, or low?

Possible Links
Officers, board members, staff:

What is our history or prior relationship with this institution?

How to Apply for Support
State the source of the following information: the prospect's giving guidelines, directory profile, or other source:

Does the institution have its own application form?

TO-DO EXERCISE 11.4, continued

Does it accept a regional grantmaking organization's form?

Does it require an initial letter of inquiry or can we submit the full proposal?

What are the deadlines?

Have we checked the following?

_____ Annual report

_____ Giving guidelines

_____ Grant directories and indexes

_____ 990PF

Corporate Sponsorship
Does a significant opportunity exist?

How does the population we serve match the population the corporation is trying to reach?

How would aligning with our program benefit the corporation?

Notes and Ranking
On the basis of *capacity, commitment,* and *connection,* what is this prospect's overall rank (A1 through C3):

Balinese music or a group of volunteers counseling children in a shelter, your proposal has only a brief opportunity to make its case before they have to move on to the next proposal.

One Midwestern foundation officer showed us a proposal for six religious, ethnic, and educational institutions to work together to start an after-school tutoring program for immigrant Latino students. A worthy cause? It certainly sounded like one, but the proposal left her confused about which organizations should receive the check.

We asked this foundation officer what happens to requests that are difficult to understand. "We don't toss them away when we sense there is substance to them," she said. "We put them aside and plan to follow up later. But you know there's never enough time to reconsider as many of them as we'd like."

Eight Avoidable Errors

Here are eight undesirable, but common, reactions to fundraising requests, each of which addresses a key piece of information you need to present in your proposal. Each reaction is followed by a suggestion for avoiding the error that caused it.

1. "I read the proposal twice and still don't understand it." Follow the suggestions in Chapter Five and To-Do Exercise 5.4 for polishing your answers to the six questions donors ask, so you can write a professional presentation that highlights the merits of your project.

2. "It's not clear what this nonprofit does." What's your mission? State it briefly and clearly.

3. "Why did this nonprofit contact me?" Does your mission fit in with the institution's charitable purpose? If so, tell the people reading your proposal why your organization is a perfect fit. If it's not a perfect fit, don't waste your time or theirs *unless* you have a high-level friend who is closely connected to the funder's board. In that case have your contact introduce your organization's funding request.

4. "What distinguishes this funding request?" What makes your project special? Do you have a more effective way, for example, of feeding the hungry? Emphasize why your project is compelling so the person evaluating your request will never ask this question.

5. "Is this request from a certified not-for-profit organization?" Most foundations and corporations make grants only to organizations with not-for-profit legal status. Be sure to prove your group is a legit-

imate 501(c)(3) organization by including a copy of its IRS letter of determination.

6. "Is this nonprofit credible?" Once interested in your cause, an institutional donor will want to look at who else is backing it, who else is supporting your efforts. Will the person reading your request know any of these supporters? Include a packet of supporter reference information to add indispensable credibility to your organization and its project.

7. "How much do they want?" How much money is needed to make your project happen? You don't want to low-ball your request, but neither do you want to ask for an excessive amount. Include a project budget that supports your request for a specific amount.

8. "This is the first I've heard from the people at this nonprofit since we funded them last year." Keep all donors including institutional donors apprised of your project and your organization. As obvious as this sounds, you need a follow-up plan in order to avoid giving donors that love-'em-and-leave-'em feeling and to ease their way to funding your worthy cause in the future.

Further Reading on Grantwriting

Ruskin, K. B., and Achilles, C. M. *Grantwriting, Fundraising, and Partnerships: Strategies That Work!* Thousand Oaks, Calif.: Corwin Press, 1995.

Part Four

Putting the Plan Together

Chapter 12

What Your Fundraising Plan Looks Like

YOUR FUNDRAISING PLAN is a map and itinerary for raising the money your nonprofit needs to carry out its objectives. It has a flexible design; you will alter it as your needs change and as you obtain new information. We assemble the plan in this chapter and present a variety of forms it can take. The look of your specific plan, like its contents, will depend on how your nonprofit operates and where it wants to focus its energy.

The physical plan comprises four parts:

1. Fundraising overview: shows the projections of how much your organization needs to raise along with a list of donors and prospects and targeted giving objectives that meet the funding need.

2. Fundraising activity schedules: show the steps required for each fundraising activity and major prospect solicitation to occur.

3. Calendars: show when the various steps in events, mailings, and other fundraising activities will occur. Calendars are derived from the fundraising schedules; you may have both calendars for specific activities and a master calendar that shows the plan overview and all schedule information.

4. Progress reports: monitor the pulse of your plan. They compare actual results with projected outcomes so you can encourage activities that are progressing well and intervene in those that are lagging behind.

We described in Chapter Four how to carry out a fundraising overview. In this chapter we discuss activity schedules and calendars, and then we examine follow-up activities in Chapter Thirteen.

The Overview Plan

As we described in Chapter Four, the overview of your fundraising plan takes a broad look at the areas where you plan to raise money and estimates how much will be raised from each. The overview plan you worked on in Chapter Four helped prepare you to select the appeals you would use and the donors and prospects you would approach. However, you did not enter that information on a timeline. Now it's time to take a look at the individual tasks necessary to reach your overview goals, and to fit them into a timeframe. As an example we'll use the PTA fundraising overview from Chapter Four and show how the PTA might expand it with activity schedules.

Exhibit 12.1 reviews the initial version of the PTA's overview for funding its after-school program. It is shown here as it looks entered into Outlook, a scheduling program that comes bundled with some versions of Microsoft Office. The *categories* are the areas in which the PTA plans to raise money. Each *activity* is a means to accomplish part of the goal.

Fundraising Activity Schedules

Without a recipe you might not remember all the ingredients you need to make your favorite meal. Without a fundraising activity schedule, you

---

EXHIBIT 12.1

Overview Funding Plan: PTA After-School Program.

OVERVIEW FUNDING PLAN: PTA After-School Program

	Subject	Status	Due Date	Person Responsible
Categories : Companies $7.15M				
Activity : Ads $3,150				
Activity : Banks $4,000				
Categories : Fundraisers $13-$16M				
Activity : Dinner/Dance $10,000				
Activity : Phonathon $3 - 6,000				
Categories : Other $500				
Activity : Bake Sale $500				
Categories : PTA Members $12M				
Activity : Large Member Gifts $2,000				
Activity : Member Requests $10,000				

Source: *Screen shots from* Outlook *and* Microsoft Office *reprinted by permission of Microsoft Corporation.* Outlook *and* Microsoft Office *are registered trademarks of Microsoft Corporation, which owns all rights and copyrights related to such products. Copyright © 1999 by Microsoft Corporation.*

might leave out the most important tasks needed to raise funds from a particular donor group.

An activity schedule is made up of the key ingredients needed for the fundraising activity to occur. The PTA planned a dinner-dance for May, for example. To succeed with this event, the three people in charge knew they needed to form a committee, decide on a theme, and carry out such other tasks as hiring a band, designing and sending out invitations, and publicizing the event. They decided on a date for a dinner-dance strategy meeting at which they could go over what steps were needed, when they should be completed, and by whom.

Writing down each step stimulates an understanding of what's needed to accomplish the whole activity. The resulting schedules form the nucleus of a fundraising plan. If you've ever jotted down a to-do list or created a tickler file, then you have already experienced this. You write down only those things you think are necessary. Of course activity schedules, like to-do lists, can be added to and updated throughout the planning cycle.

Each fundraising activity schedule should include:

1. The *point person* who is in charge of the activity (although the ultimate person in charge is you or maybe an assistant)
2. The *financial goal*
3. The *targeted donor prospects*
4. The specific *fundraising strategy* to be used

Determining Fundraising Tasks

Monday morning you walk into your office, hit a button on the computer, and up pops a reminder: "Begin proposal for XYZ Foundation; it's due in 3 weeks. Schedule prospect luncheon with Mrs. Boyd." How does that happen? The reason is that you input all those tasks days, weeks, or months earlier. Those tasks are the basic units of your fundraising activity schedules and your calendars.

The heart of fundraising planning is determining the essential activities large and small that lead up to securing contributions and establishing when they have to occur and who will do them—meeting the submission deadlines for grant applications; remembering and marking the anniversaries of major gifts; writing letters and other materials for fall, winter, spring and summer mailings; completing all the preparations for special events on time, making preparations for effective board meetings, and so forth. These essential activities will be the building blocks of your plan—the research, cultivation, and solicitation activities that need doing.

Taking the fundraising categories and activities from the overview, you will note the work that needs to be done for each fundraising activity to occur, such as

- Identifying the individual and institutional prospects most likely to give to your worthy cause.

- Planning your prospect cultivation and solicitation activities.

- Estimating how long each activity will take; get these estimates, preferably, from the people directly responsible for doing the activity.

- Linking related activities: for example, because grant writing can't start until grant research finishes, link these two activities so their time estimates will be added together.

- Entering grant application deadlines, major donor gift anniversaries, board meeting times, and other fixed dates.

As you do this, you will produce detailed activity schedules of what needs to be done each week to prepare to meet your deadlines. Later this information will be used on your planning calendar. So the more accurate the activities list the better. But don't be overly worried that your first planning efforts have to be 100 percent accurate. The planning process is more like making a series of drafts than producing a final report. Each draft is based on the best information you have at the moment, but as you research and gain more information, your activity schedule will change and grow more detailed and complete.

Using Task Notecards

We suggest that you write up a notecard that describes each fundraising task, breaking the steps of each activity down to a practical level of detail. If you list fundraising tasks that are trivial, you will clutter up your plan with too much detail and, as the saying goes, "not be able to see the forest for the trees." If you don't put in enough detail, then you may forget steps necessary for the activity to be successfully completed. As you become experienced in preparing activity schedules, you will find a balance between citing too much information and oversimplifying.

For example, "send out newsletter," is too large a project to be listed as one task. Why? Because it's not a single action but dependent on several previous actions. Before an organization can send out a newsletter, articles need to be written, photos chosen, copy laid out, mailing lists selected, printing done, and so on. These are the specific tasks that would be included in an activity schedule for a newsletter.

Conversely, "stuff newsletters into envelopes" is probably too small to be listed as a separate activity on the fundraising plan. It's a customary part of the task of mailing the newsletters.

The main thing to remember is that the steps in each fundraising activity should be well defined, precise, and detailed. And they must also be significant, like the tasks that people put on their to-do lists. They note things that will measurably move the fundraising process forward.

You should also consider the mechanics of producing task notecards. Handwritten or typed cards are certainly practical and sufficient for many fundraising activities, however, you can also use computer software to do the job. Scheduling software includes task notecard forms such as the one in Exhibit 12.2, which shows a task notecard for a meeting to prepare a PTA membership mailing scheduled for March 1. Volunteers are going to stuff, address, and stamp envelopes. The goal is to raise $10,000 through requests to PTA members.

As Exhibit 12.2 shows, the computerized task notecard has a *subject* field where you can write the name of the task, a due date or range of dates field, and an open area to jot down notes on what you want to accomplish, who will be responsible, and so forth. You can use the *category* field for the name of the overview funding area that the task relates to. The next page of the task notecard (not shown here) has space to name the fundraising activity the task is a part of. (We'll describe more of the benefits and drawbacks of scheduling software later in the chapter.)

Using Activity Schedules to Expand Your Plan Overview

You can use the information on your completed activity schedules to expand your fundraising overview to a higher level of detail. Exhibit 12.3 illustrates the PTA overview as it looked after the activity schedules were drawn up and the tasks from those schedules were entered into the overview. Each *subject* is the name of a fundraising task. When you double-click on a subject, it brings up the task notecard for that subject, such as the one in Exhibit 12.2. You can update the information or refresh your memory of task details at any time.

Assigning Activity Schedules

If you are the only staff person handling fundraising for your organization, you can put together the activity lists and schedules on your own.

EXHIBIT 12.2

Computerized Task Notecard.

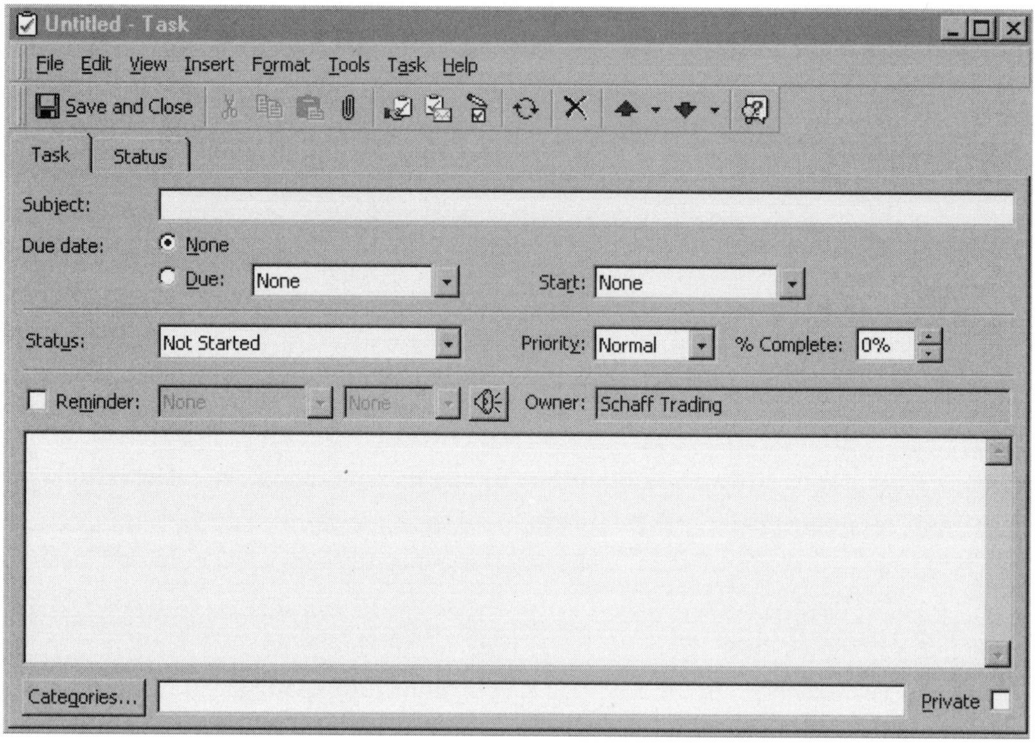

Source: *Screen shots from Outlook and Microsoft Office reprinted by permission of Microsoft Corporation. Outlook and Microsoft Office are registered trademarks of Microsoft Corporation, which owns all rights and copyrights related to such products. Copyright © 1999 by Microsoft Corporation.*

But if you have a number of people working on raising funds for your organization, you will want to ask each of them to prepare activities lists and schedules that you can add to your master plan. That way your organization will have a complete picture of all its fundraising activities.

Everyone who handles an area, such as individual giving, corporate and foundation giving, or government grants, should be familiar with the specific fundraising actions that are required. But by preparing activities lists and schedules everyone will also be forced to take a fresh look at his or her area and, in the process, may find some solicitations and appeals have fallen through the cracks or have been carried out inadequately.

Exactly what kind of information are you collecting for your master schedule? From the person in charge of government grants, you should get a list of RFP (request for proposal) due dates, and the projects for which your organization is submitting proposals. The person in charge of government grants compiles very detailed statistical information and lengthy

EXHIBIT 12.3

PTA Overview Funding Plan: Expanded View.

Categories Companies $7.15M
    Activity Ads $3,150
        Subject Due 2/22/99 - Contact Newspapers to Donate Space
        Subject Due 3/10/99 - Ask local Artist to Design Logo & Ad
        Subject Due 3/22/99 - Contact local businesses to buy Ads
        Subject Due 5/2/99 - "Thank you" ad hits local papers
    Activity Banks $4,000
        Subject Due 3/1/99 - Plan Cultivation & Solicitation of Banks
        Subject Due 3/15/99 - Request meeting with Bank Contacts
        Subject Due 3/18/99 - Send Bank Contacts letter and program packet
        Subject Due 4/1/99 - In-person Solicitation of Banks
        Subject Due 4/5/99 - Follow-up with Bank Contacts
Categories Fundraisers $13-$16M
    Activity Dinner/Dance $10,000
        Subject Due 12/21/98 - Strategy Meeting - Form Committee
        Subject Due 2/1/99 - Committee Meeting
        Subject Due 2/1/99 - Hire Band
        Subject Due 2/15/99 - Invitations are designed
        Subject Due 3/1/99 - Invitations sent to printer
        Subject Due 3/15/99 - Committee Meeting
        Subject Square Dance Held 5/15/99
    Activity Phonathon $3 - 6,000
        Subject Due 1/15/99 Meeting - Organize Helpers
        Subject Due 3/15/99 Draft Phonathon Script; Train Helpers
        Subject Due 4/1/99 Hold Phonathon
        Subject Due 9/15/99 Hold 2nd Phonathon, if necessary
Categories Other $500
    Activity Bake Sale $500
        Subject Due 1/29/99 - Get Concession Space at Craft Fair
        Subject Due 4/30/99 - Organize Bake Sale
        Subject Due 5/22/99 - Hold Bake Sale at annual Craft Fair
Categories PTA Members $12M
    Activity Large Member Gifts $2,000
        Subject Due 1/15/99 - Ask 2 Others for $500
        Subject Due 1/22/99 - Collect Pledges
    Activity Member Requests $10,000
        Subject Due 1/10/99 - Meeting to Organize Mailing
        Subject Due 2/11/99 - Draft Mailing & Approve
        Subject Due 3/1/99 - Meeting to Prepare Mailing
        Subject Due 3/9/99 - Send out Mailing for After-School Program

Source: *Screen shots from* Outlook *and* Microsoft Office *reprinted by permission of Microsoft Corporation.* Outlook *and* Microsoft Office *are registered trademarks of Microsoft Corporation, which owns all rights and copyrights related to such products. Copyright © 1999 by Microsoft Corporation.*

descriptive material because that is what government grants require. One of the benefits of putting RFP dates on the master schedule is that other areas know they can then reference the wealth of data contained in the completed RFPs for their own appeals.

From the corporate and foundation person, you should get a schedule of priorities—last year's results, this year's projections, and a schedule of corporate and foundation solicitations. You should get the same kind of information for your master schedule from the person overseeing individual giving.

This process of sharing activities lists can be very helpful in another way. It not only produces your master schedule but it can suggest ways for the people involved with raising individual, corporate, foundation, and government funds to begin working together more effectively. When everyone is working away on her own area, it is easy to become somewhat isolated from others. Sharing information counteracts that tendency.

For smaller nonprofits another way to get started is to assemble a giant tickler file, by month, slipping in pieces of donor and prospect correspondence showing which foundation, corporation, or individual needs to be solicited, thanked, approached, cultivated, or given a report. This is a very practical approach to developing schedules. Say a report is needed on a certain date: stick a piece of paper in the tickler file with that information highlighted, putting it in the folder for the month when it's time to begin the report. This is one way to operate effectively without software.

Reminders

To create an effective list of fundraising activities to go on your calendar, use the following rules:

- Include only activities that are critical for each appeal or donor.

- Make sure activities are significant but also capable of completion in a short time compared to the time needed to complete the overall appeal (very large activities might be better defined as two activities, for example).

- Remember to include tasks that occur repetitively, such as board meetings, status reports, and anticipated revision work.

Fundraising Calendars

A fundraising calendar is a timetable for mailings, benefits, and other fundraising activities. Putting the activities and tasks defined in the activity schedules on a calendar helps ensure you won't get behind on any of them. An annual calendar can act as a flowchart of activities for the whole year. When you lay out this timetable of your mailings, events, cultivations, and solicitations, you will see whether you have too many activities scheduled or whether you have gaps where little is planned. You will be able to make adjustments early so that your schedule of activities will go smoothly and effectively.

It's useful to have an open mind about what your calendar can look like. For nonprofits that use a variety of methods to raise money, it's often helpful to see upcoming fundraising activities in different ways. What kind of planning calendar should you use? That depends on what kind of information you want to work with. Today you might want to focus on this week's deadlines. Tomorrow you might want to step back and see what's scheduled for the next six months. Part of the popularity of scheduling and calendar software is that you can output data the way you want—in daily, weekly, or monthly formats. Selecting the calendar format that best suits your needs can help you perform your development tasks more efficiently.

An event like a benefit may warrant its own calendar. If a benefit takes place in January, the benefit committee may need to be formed four months earlier. The mailings to join the benefit committee must be sent out by a certain date. The invitations must be printed by a particular date and sent out by another (see the calendar for the PTA barbecue-square dance in Exhibit 12.4). A nonprofit with substantial mailings, such as a college, will have a calendar just for mailings. Still, a small organization may well be able to use only a master calendar listing all its fundraising activities and tasks, and skip the step of creating separate calendars as well.

In addition, separate calendars can be made for each donor area (individuals, corporations, foundations, and government sources). Again, these separate calendars should be tied into a master calendar that shows the complete picture. In a smaller nonprofit this can be done manually, but if you have scheduling software, calendars can be linked so that information entered on one will be automatically placed on another as well.

For smaller nonprofits a large monthly calendar and some colored pencils may be sufficient to provide a flowchart of the development activities to be done. It could be a plastic calendar, the kind you can write on and wipe off. A larger organization will probably use a calendar with columns of days or weeks divided into rows for writing in multiple key fundraising activities such as events, mailings, and solicitation calls. Choose the calendar format that lets you view the data you want.

EXHIBIT 12.4

PTA Barbecue-Square Dance Calendar.

Activity	Due By	Persons Involved	Person Responsible	Notes
Strategy meeting	12/21	Michael Caine Susan Leuchs Mary Brenner Judy Rice	MC, SL	Agenda: 1. Timetable for event 2. Financial goal 3. Cochair candidates 4. Strategy for publicity
Research bands	1/15	MC, JR	JR	Follow-up on suggestions
Committee meetings	2/1	MC, SL, JR, Lucy Friedman	SL	1. Menu options 2. Activities & entertainment 3. Responsibilities
Hire band	2/2	JR	JR	Larry Talbot to review contract
Invitations designed	2/15	SL, MC, LF, Trudy Baldwin	SL	
Committee meeting	3/1	SL, MC, MB, JR, LF	SL	
Invitations sent to printer	3/3	JR		
Committee meeting	3/17	SL, MC, MB, JR, LF	SL	
Invitations mailed	3/29	LF		
Barbecue-square dance held	5/12			

Exhibit 12.5 shows a simple calendar that lets you see the names of the fundraising activities planned for a specific timeframe (week, month, or year). Such calendars are useful for conducting overviews, handing out at meetings, and taping to the wall.

Here are some calendar reminders. Put the following information on your calendar so your fundraising plan stays on track:

- Grant application deadlines.
- Mailings.
- Fundraising calls to major donors.
- Cultivation events, such as breakfasts, lunches, and receptions.
- Phonathons.
- Benefits.
- Board meetings.
- Gift anniversaries of your major donors (for example, if someone gave in May, make sure the next solicitation goes out in February, at least three months in advance).

When to Design Your Plan

Start designing your fundraising plan toward the start of your fiscal year. Review last year's results to help schedule this year's fundraising activities. If your fiscal year begins in July, in May and June you should be evaluating what happened in the year that's coming to a close so you can do your planning for the next year over June, July, and August. Based on the analysis you have done, craft the fundraising strategies you will use for your next fiscal year. By August you should be marking on the calendar foundation and corporate grant application deadlines, big events, anniversary dates of gifts, and other important dates. Fill in what you have to do to get the fall mailing out. You'll want to launch another mailing in February or March for people who didn't give in December, so mark that down. If you're fundraising nationally, when do you think you'll take your Midwest trip, your West Coast trip, and so on?

Try to have your fundraising plan ready before September because you're going to be busy then approaching individuals for contributions and preparing grant proposals with application deadlines that month and in October. After that, it's a mad dash to year's end. Individual donors have different giving cycles, but a crucial one to prepare for is December

EXHIBIT 12.5

PTA March Calendar for After-School Program Fundraising Activities.

March 1999

	April 1999					
	S	M	T	W	T	F	S
	4	5	6	7	1	2	3
	11	12	13	14	8	9	10
	18	19	20	21	15	16	17
	25	26	27	28	22	23	24
					29	30	

Monday	Tuesday	Wednesday	Thursday	Friday	Sat/Sun
March 1 Banks cultivation meeting D/Dance meeting	2	3 D/Dance invites to printer	4 Meeting to prepare mailing	5	6
8	9 Ads - Ask local artist to design	10	11	12	7
15 Bank contacts - request appts	16	17 D/Dance meeting	18 Followup - Bank contacts	19	13
22	23 Ads - contact local business	24	25	26	14 Send out mailing for after-school
29 D/Dance invites mailed	30	31	April 1 In-person bank solicitation 6:00pm Phonathon	2	20
				3	21
				4	27
					28
					3
					4

31. For tax reasons, the bulk of contributions from individuals comes in around then.

Exhibit 12.6 illustrates a hypothetical fundraising schedule for an organization operating on a July 1 to June 30 fiscal year.

Now work out a fundraising activity schedule and calendar for one of your organization's fundraising methods (To-Do Exercise 12.1).

Scheduling, Calendar, and Project Software

You don't need software to produce schedules or to make calendars, but if your organization is large enough or its fundraising is complex enough, the right software can make the process easier. Even if you already have a donor records software package, you can benefit by adding a scheduling and calendar program to it. That's because most development software is database oriented. It focuses on compiling donor and giving information and does not have much scheduling or calendar software built in. With the donor records software Raiser's Edge, for example, you can add *action reminders* to donor records. They are useful; you can, for example, pull regular reports of anyone with open actions. But you cannot transfer that information to a calendar program.

When it comes to choosing scheduling and calendar software, there simply is not one package that does it all well. Specific calendar software, such as Calendar Creator by Softkey, sells for under $50. It produces great calendars but does not do as good a job with schedules. Outlook does a good job with tasks and schedules. It is included with Microsoft Office, including the upgrade versions, or you can buy it separately for around $100. It also comes bundled with other software. Programs like Outlook can be networked to help users communicate.

Outlook's calendars could be functionally improved, but overall Outlook is a very useful program. You can get as detailed as you want. It's easy to link the activity schedules to calendars. For example, after you specify the tasks for your various fundraising activities, the software can then rearrange those data into one overall calendar.

Here are some pluses and minuses of the three software types you might be considering:

- Development software tracks donors, gift histories, and progress toward fundraising goals but does not provide scheduling and calendar capabilities. Examples: Banner, Benefactor, Results Plus, Raiser's Edge.

- Scheduling and calendar software produces fundraising schedules and calendars but can't interface directly with donor records. Examples: Lotus Organizer, Microsoft Outlook.

- Project management software allows you to create subcalendars that link to master calendars and provides some calendar formats that other software don't have, but it's expensive and not geared toward the needs of smaller nonprofits. Examples: Microsoft Project, ASTA PowerProject.

EXHIBIT 12.6

Sample Fiscal Year Fundraising Schedule.

July	Analyze last year's results. Based on that analysis, develop a plan for the coming year.
	Schedule benefit for the following spring.
	Over the summer come up with a theme, an honoree, and a benefit chairman.
August	Schedule fundraising events for the coming year.
	Begin drafting September fundraising letters to donors and prospects.
	Schedule donor and prospect visits (at least one a week).
September	Convene development committee, assign responsibilities, discuss fundraising goals.
	Send out a short informative letter to donors and prospects about the institution's activities. Enclose donor reply form and a return envelope.
	Form a benefit committee. Look for a corporate or individual underwriter for the event. Ask benefit committee members to supply lists of friends to invite to benefit.
October	Get commitments from all board members of their contributions for the coming year.
	Send out at least one grant proposal a week to a corporation or foundation, based on research and contact responses.
	Hold cultivation breakfast or lunch hosted by a board member.
	Send out follow-up letters to attendees of the cultivation event.
	Send renewal gift reminders to individual donors 2–3 months prior to the anniversary of their gifts.
	Benefit committee meets. Each member of the committee is asked to buy a table at the benefit (if it is a dinner or a lunch).
November	Send out year-end mailing to individual donors, lapsed donors, and selected prospects.
	Get a corporate contributor to host cultivation luncheon or breakfast for corporations and foundations at the contributor's offices.
	Send out follow-up letters requesting support after the event or make follow-up calls and/or schedule follow-up visits to request support.

EXHIBIT 12.6 (continued)

Sample Fiscal Year Fundraising Schedule.

	Schedule phonathon to telephone all individual donors to ask for renewal of their support. (Do not call donors who have given within the last two months.)
	Development Committee meets, reviews progress, decides if progress is satisfactory, and takes on new responsibilities.
December	Continue visiting donors and prospects (at least one a week) on cultivation calls and to request funds.
January	Do a six-month analysis of results.
	Call donors who have not responded to the year-end mailing or draft a short reminder note to them.
	Continue visiting donors and prospects.
	Development Committee meets, looks at fundraising results, takes on new assignments. If there are board members whose gifts remain outstanding, either the Chairman of the Development Committee or Chairman of the Board will take on the responsibility of obtaining those gifts.
	Benefit committee meets, benefit invitation copy is finalized, a master guest list is formed.
February	Benefit invitations are addressed and sent.
	Proposals sent at least once a week to major prospects.
	Second corporate and foundation cultivation events held at corporate or foundation donor's office or hosted by board member or held at organization.
	Newsletters or informational mailing sent to donors and prospects describing organization's activities and needs, reply cards enclosed and return envelopes.
	Weekly cultivation and solicitation calls continue to individuals, foundations, and corporations.
March	Benefit event held.
	Follow-up thank-you's sent to all benefit donors, and benefit committee members.
	Fiscal year-end mailing drafted to individuals, list of names generated, and dollar requests assigned.
	Development committee meets, reviews results, takes on new assignments.
April	Fiscal year-end mailing sent to all donors (except ones that have given during the last 2–3 months).
	Cultivation and solicitation calls continue.
	Proposals drafted and sent to selected major donors.
May	Development Committee meets to discuss last push for year-end funding and to review fundraising results.
	Delinquent donors are called and asked to renew their gifts.
	Initial planning begins for next year's fundraising campaign.
June	Wrap up on all outstanding funds needed.

TO-DO EXERCISE 12.1

Creating a Fundraising Activity Schedule and Calendar

1. Choose one way your nonprofit raises funds and write out the key activities and tasks of this method. Take mailings, for example. Say you want donors and prospects to receive four mailings a year. What activities are required to get these appeals out? You would schedule a September solicitation mailing to let people know what your organization is doing this year, and then another mailing in late fall that gets to people in time for year-end giving. You would update your donors in February. And in May you would write to them again before your fiscal year ends in June. Then you would determine the steps necessary to accomplish each of these mailings and put them into a timeframe.

2. Take your list of fundraising activities and select a calendar to display them. Transfer the activities to the calendar.

Part Five

Monitoring the Plan

Chapter 13

Evaluating Your Progress and Following Up

YOUR FUNDRAISING PLAN is designed to organize the steps necessary to raise funds for your organization. If that were all you used it for, though, you would gain only a part of its real benefit. You will also want use it to monitor your progress. By preparing status reports comparing current results to those projected in your plan, you will be able to see where things are going well, and you will make sure you address areas that lag behind. You will also be able to check planned fundraising activities against those already carried out and, if necessary, change the next steps of your campaign. As this chapter describes, the reports themselves are not hard to produce, but require you to keep your plan current.

Understanding the Benefits of Progress Reports

The way for development committee members to keep a pulse on the fundraising campaign is through regular progress, or status, reports. These confidential reports can be selectively circulated to specific board members (such as the members of the board development committee) or presented to top administrators for action. They can be used in one-to-one discussions or as topics for a group meeting. By keeping your board members and other volunteers up to date, these reports help you keep them motivated and give them an incentive to stay productive.

Because evaluating your progress also keeps you honest about activities accomplished and their results, it should be done at least once a month. If your organization already has a track record, you have something to measure your progress against. You will measure progress compared with what you need and estimates you have made. For instance, you can compare last year's results by a particular time against this year's. How many donors repeated their gifts, how many increased them, and how many were new contributors? What was the total raised last year? What was the average gift? How do those numbers compare to this year's results?

Regular reporting allows you to change course while there's still time. Consider the situation a New York nonprofit was in when a major corporate donor changed its giving priorities and dramatically reduced its support. The organization's development staff looked ahead and decided they could not count on getting the big infusion of cash from individuals or other corporations that would be needed to fill the gap by year's end. They also knew they needed to act fast. Maybe another funding proposal would come through, but it wasn't prudent to count on that. They decided they had to begin immediate planning for a benefit. Five months later a cocktail party with music, dancing, and a silent auction was held in the nonprofit's honor at a recently redone consulate, and it was a resounding success. Two companies sponsored and underwrote the event. The benefit provided the final monies needed for the organization's programs.

To summarize, tracking your progress helps you reach your fundraising goals in these four ways:

- Comparing contribution estimates against actual dollars raised allows you to quickly respond to changing conditions. You can replace funding sources, go after new prospects, and otherwise alter donor or appeal strategies.

- Tracking completion of key fundraising activities lets you zero in on what needs to be done to complete cultivation and solicitation assignments. You won't forget a key step in an appeal.

- Producing status reports for board members, development staff, and key fundraising participants informs, involves, and helps motivate them to carry out assignments and take on new responsibilities.

- Maintaining original and updated fundraising plans helps you conduct effective postmortems of the current year's campaign—what went well and why, and what flopped and what you can do to avoid a repeat, so that next year's campaign will be even more productive.

Putting Together a Progress Report

A progress report contains three major sections: financial updates, status of cultivation activities, and new business.

Financial Updates

The financial updates section compares the amount of money raised so far to the estimates you made when you prepared the fundraising plan. This financial summary also shows how much remains to be raised and presents some detailed comparisons between this year and last year for, typically, repeat, new, and increased gifts; restricted and unrestricted gifts; and individual, corporate, foundation, and other gifts.

Cultivation Activities

The activity section of your status report is an update on cultivations of prospective donors. This section briefly describes the proposals and funding requests that were sent out: the date they were sent, the solicitor, the amount requested, the current status of the appeal, and the next steps necessary. It answers such questions as, Which appeals were successful and which were rejected? If one was rejected, what was the reason? Where did positive responses come from? What follow-up is necessary? A look at the outstanding tasks on the fundraising activity schedules (see Chapter Twelve) can prompt answers to these questions.

If you are planning a benefit, report on the progress made to date and what needs to be done next. If you have a board member who called on a major prospect with a funding request, add that to the report along with the next step you will take. Including such reports on cultivation activities by board members and other volunteers will help keep these people active members of nonprofit's team.

New Business

In the new business section, discuss projects and ideas that have come up since your last meeting and that could use some examination before they are added to the fundraising plan.

Exhibit 13.1 illustrates the format you could use for monthly reports on the progress of your fundraising.

Keeping Your Fundraising Plan Current

It's easy to keep your fundraising plan active, as long as you regularly update your gift information and keep your fundraising activity information current. Keeping the fundraising data current does require diligence. To make your plan an effective and valuable tool, you must input new information regularly and consistently. Enter contact information as you receive it, such as appeals received by the donor or prospect and cultivations visits

EXHIBIT 13.1

Format for a Monthly Fundraising Progress Report.

Monthly Fundraising Progress Report: September

Contributions Received This Year **As of September 30th**	**Contributions Received Last Year** **As of September 30th**

Number of Donors & Gift Amounts	Number of Donors & Gift Amounts
Individual Corp. Fdn. Other	Individual Corp. Fdn. Other
Repeat donors	Repeat donors
Increased donors	Increased donors
New donors	New donors
Recovered donors	Recovered donors
Total	Total
Unrestricted gifts	Unrestricted gifts
Restricted gifts	Restricted gifts

Activity Report

Individuals

New requests. State that during the month of September funding requests were sent to the following individuals, for the following projects, requesting the following amounts of money. Next steps and/or necessary follow-up are given in each case.

Requests outstanding. State that the organization has outstanding requests to the following individuals, for the following projects, requesting the following amounts of money. Next steps and/or necessary follow-up are given in each case.

Positive responses. State that positive responses to funding requests were received from the following individuals for the following reasons. Next steps are given in each case.

Negative responses. State that negative responses were received from the following individuals for the following reasons. Next steps are given in each case.

Corporations

Follow the format for individuals.

Foundations

Follow the format for individuals. Tie in deadlines for proposal submissions to the progress meeting schedule, to check progress.

Benefits and Other Fundraising Events

Give a status report on the action taken and the next steps needed.

that have occurred. Record gifts received. Add this information to your fundraising activity schedules, and check off tasks as they are completed. This information you are compiling is what you will use to produce your progress reports.

The best way to stay on top of data collection is to stick to a regular schedule. Enter contributions data every day a gift is received (in a gifts ledger or a donor database), check off task completions, and enter call reports. Check once a week to see if activity lists need updating. Decide on the procedure that best suits your organization, and keep it as simple as the needs of your campaign allow. The easier your methods of data collection, the more likely you are to get the information you need in a timely manner.

If your campaign is small, you will pull together the data you need yourself. For more complex fundraising, the individuals responsible for each appeal or area can compile data and give them to you on paper or by entering them in a computer network you have access to, relieving you of one time-consuming task. Those closest to the work know best the status of that work.

In a large nonprofit you probably have no choice but to get information from others. Still, you'll need to spot-check information for accuracy. And you or another staff member will still have to generate the progress reports after the data have been entered in the computer system. However, once you have chosen the format for your first report, you should be able to easily call up the subsequent monthly updates. Many gift management software packages come with a number of "canned" reports, basic development formats that you can tailor for your purposes and easily update to produce series of reports.

Using What Your Reports Tell You

Finding out early on what the discrepancies are between your projections and what is actually occurring allows you to adjust your strategies and to head off potential underfunding before it becomes critical. The variances to look for when comparing your results to the original plan include

- Appeals that are not bringing in what was expected

- Donors who gave last year but not yet this year

- Prospects who haven't yet been solicited

- Planned fundraising activities that are not starting or finishing on time

• Cultivation and solicitation activities that require more time than scheduled

Variances from your plan aren't always bad; they can highlight good news as well as bad. A higher return than projected on a fundraising appeal is good news but is also worth looking into. That is, the results of each fundraising appeal need to be examined, not just the results of the overall campaign, if you are to maximize total contributions. For example, if your fall mailing brings in 20 percent more than last year, is that increase due to an increase in average gift size or an increase in the number of donors? Should you expect the results of your winter mailing to be reduced because some portion of those who gave as a result of last winter's appeal responded earlier this year, giving to the fall appeal?

What if solicitation results are lower than expected? In that case, find out what's causing the shortfall. In which areas is fundraising behind? With which constituencies? Which appeals?

Reports Explain Shortfalls and Windfalls

Detailed reports can help you respond dynamically to funding challenges. As you break down the total contributions received by different categories of donor groups (individuals, corporations, foundations, and others) and by types of gifts, you will discover what area or individuals need attention.

At the fiscal year halfway point, a social services group was behind by 10 percent ($43,000) in total individual contributions compared to the previous year. Which sector was underperforming? The traditional appeals were going fine, so the development director wondered if major donors might be lagging. This nonprofit defined major donors as those giving $500 or more. So to find out, he ran a LYBUNT (Last Year But Not This Year) report, looking at donors who had given over $500 last year to see if this group was underperforming. It turned out that major donors were $55,000 behind! That is, last year by this time, major donors had contributed $55,000 more than they had this year. Not only did the LYBUNT report uncover the source of the 10 percent shortfall (the major donor group), it pointed out where to look for these funds—among the major donors who had missed their anniversaries. The nonprofit followed up with these donors and recovered nearly the whole shortfall in the second half of the fiscal year.

By the way, the difference of $12,000 between the nonprofit's shortfall ($43,000) and the amount expected but overdue from major donors

($55,000) was mostly accounted for by the new donor report, which showed almost $10,500 in new gifts over $500.

More than likely, at some point in your fundraising campaign, you will want to analyze donor giving histories to explain actual funding results as compared to what you expected. Donor software such as Benefactor and Raiser's Edge offers a wide variety of preformatted report choices, from reports on matching gifts, gifts-in-kind, and pledges to reports that rate the performance of solicitors. Exhibits 13.2, 13.3, 13.4, and 13.5 are examples of the kinds of detailed reports (compiled with Raiser's Edge) that can help you uncover the reasons behind contribution shortfalls and windfalls:

Reports Are a Reality Check

Your fundraising plan is not a rigid structure. It can be adapted to your specific situation. If your initial prospect for a $25,000 gift doesn't pan out, and you don't have another prospect at that level, look for two prospects who could give $12,500 each. If you don't have two prospects for $12,500 gifts, do you have five possible $5,000 gifts?

What choices are available to you for adjusting your plan to accommodate the differences between your original funding estimates and what's actually coming in? You can

- Add on new appeals or redesign old ones
- Assign additional fundraising staff to help with fundraising activities not yet completed
- Assist solicitors
- Adjust program budgets

All nonprofits need to be ready to alter their plans to meet unforeseen events. If fundraising goals are not met, programs may have to change or be postponed. That's a possibility virtually all nonprofits face that operate without endowment funds. If a gap develops between the expenses you've budgeted and the money you bring in, something has to give. If fundraising alternatives are exhausted, the safety valve has to be program changes, unless you have a patron saint or genie you can count on to rescue you. A word of advice on patron saints and genies, however—get them to make firm commitments sooner rather than later. Unrealistic financial expectations can be dangerous and can lead to severe program adjustments, even bankruptcy.

To-Do Exercise 13.1 will get you started on designing your monthly report.

EXHIBIT 13.2

Sample LYBUNT Report.

Start Date: 01/01/95 End Date: 12/31/95

Constituent Name	Last Gift	Date
Jorn S. Chapman 78 West View Drive #26 Summerville, SC 29420	300.00	1/15/94
Mark J. Gaines 1207 Leeds Avenue Charleston, SC 29401	2,000.00	11/12/94
Benjamin C. Grant 2301 Palm Parkway Hilton Head, SC 29498	150.00	1/24/94
Karen D. Haggard 1205 Park Place New York, NY 30391	50.00	1/13/94
Harold H. Hicks 1233 South Del Norte Drive Loveland, CO 30389	75.00	1/15/94
John Lanning 2600 St. Michael's Boulevard Boston, MA 02110	50.00	4/10/94
Francine M. Romero 538 Stoneledge Drive Boston, MA 02110	75.00	4/15/94
Mary A. Smith 34 Oakmont Drive Charleston, SC 29445	100.00	1/15/94
Anthony M. Snyder #9 Indigo Lane Summerville, SC 29854	500.00	8/12/94
Marie Woods 1011 North Bridge Boulevard Goose Creek, 29445	275.00	9/18/94
10 Constituent(s) Listed	3,575.00	

EXHIBIT 13.3

Sample Comparative Report.

5/15/95   **Anson Heritage Foundation**   Page 1
                                          Comparative Report

From Group: Alums

Constituent Name	1/1/94 5/1/94 Total Given	1/1/95 5/1/95 Total Given	Variance
Victor H. Hanson 951 Dillard Avenue Wheaton, CA 96094	0.00	185.00	185.00
Janice E. Robertson 437 Serenity Lane Mt. Pleasant, SC 29484	550.00	250.00	(300.00)
Mary E. Simpson 443 Lake Forest Drive Country Club Estates Kiawah Island, SC 29455-0443	0.00	1,000.00	1,000.00
Michael J. Simpson 443 Lake Forest Drove Country Club Estates Kiawah Island, SC 29455-0443	5,000.00	1,500.00	(3,500.00)
Rebecca B. Aaron 2344 Ruby Road Charleston, SC 29401	5,000.00	1,700.00	(3,300.00)
James M. Richards 7500 Richie Lane Brooklyn, NY 30391	3,012.00	0.00	(3,012.00)
James L. Ballou 123 Main Street Mount Pleasant, SC 29464	0.00	1,000.00	1,000.00
7 Constituent(s) Listed 3 Constituents Increased 4 Constituents Decreased	13,562.00	5,635.00	(7,927.00)

Source: The Raiser's Edge *software. The Raiser's Edge is a registered trademark of Blackbaud, Inc., which owns all rights and copyrights related to such products. © Blackbaud, Inc., 1999.*

EXHIBIT 13.4

Sample Gift Detail Report.

4/30/95 **Anson Heritage Foundation** Page 1
Gift Detail Report

Start Date: 4/1/95 End Date: 4/30/95

Constituent	Date	Fund	Cash	Stocks	Pledge Bal	MG Plg Bal	Reference
Rebecca B. Aaron	4/17/95	ANNUAL95			1,000.00		
Abernathy and Sons	4/14/95	ANNUAL95	3,000.00				
Charles Baker	4/28/95	ANNUAL95	500.00				
Myron Banks	4/14/95	ANNUAL95					
James L. Barlow	4/25/95	ANNUAL95			1,000.00		
Nancy C. Barry	4/18/95	LIBRARY	187.50				Ins of 2/16/95
	4/21/95	ANNUAL95	50.00				
Franklin A. Baymann	4/27/95	ANNUAL95	150.00				
Victor H. Hanson	4/14/95	ANNUAL95	100.00				Auction 95
Micheal B. Harold	4/15/95	ANNUAL95	500.00				Auction 95
	4/20/95	ANNUAL95	85.00				
Hillman, Marshall and Tucker	4/14/95	ANNUAL95					
Merilux	4/14/95	ANNUAL95	3,000.00				
Robert L. Norton	4/10/95	ANNUAL95	500.00				Auction 95
Jason A. Peters	4/25/95	ANNUAL95					
Maryann Peterson	4/8/95	ANNUAL95	50.00				
The Pinckney Group	4/1/95	CCPLANT	200.00				Carter Anthony Reynolds
(Robert J. Reynolds)	4/18/95	CCBUILDIN	500.00				Robert
Janice E. Robertson	4/17/95	ANNUAL95	250.00				
Romero Construction	4/14/95	ANNUAL95			3,000.00		
Mary E. Simpson	4/18/95	ANNUAL95		1,000.00			10 Shares AT&T
The City Inn	4/14/95	ANNUAL95	1,350.00				
William S. Young	4/21/95	ANNUAL95	500.00	1,000.00			

| 26 Gifts Listed | | Totals: | 11,007.50 | 1,000.00 | 5,000.00 | 0.00 | |

Source: The Raiser's Edge *software. The Raiser's Edge is a registered trademark of Blackbaud, Inc., which owns all rights and copyrights related to such products. © Blackbaud, Inc., 1999.*

EXHIBIT 13.5

Sample Gift Summary by Fund Report.

6/30/95   **Anson Heritage Foundation**   Page 1
                               Gift Summary by Fund

From Group: Annual

Start Date: 06/01/95 End Date: 06/30/95

Fund	Description	#Gifts	Cash	Stocks	Plg Balance	MG Plg Bal	Total
ANNUAL95	Annual Fund 1995	16	4,441.67	500.00	14,000.00	850.00	19,791.67
CCBUILDING	Capital Campaign Building	27	10,466.66	1,500.00	15,741.00	0.00	27,707.66
CCPLANT	Capital Campaign Plant Fund	3	2,500.00	0.00	2,500.00	0.00	5,000.00
		46	17,408.33	2,000.00	32,241.00	850.00	2,499.33

Source: The Raiser's Edge *software.* The Raiser's Edge *is a registered trademark of Blackbaud, Inc., which owns all rights and copyrights related to such products. © Blackbaud, Inc., 1999.*

TO-DO EXERCISE 13.1

Designing a Monthly Progress Report

Consider the general formats of the reports presented in this chapter and then alter one to fit your non-profit's needs. Select the key elements of your plan that you want to track. Which contribution numbers do you want regular updates on? What cultivation and solicitation activities do you regularly want to know about? Depending on your constituents and typical appeals, design a progress report to suit your organization.

Preparing for the Next Gift

Once donors have made a contribution, how you keep them informed about the project and your worthy cause will determine their continued participation. As obvious as this sounds, you need a plan to make sure it happens. Prepare an activity schedule for each major donor. Write the basic task notecards. Start with gift acknowledgment. Who should send a thank-you note or letter for a major gift? The executive director? What if a staff or volunteer solicitor was involved? When do you want the draft of the thank-you completed? Once you determine the gift acknowledgment steps, put them on a calendar and track each step.

After that, think about what next steps you will take with a major donor or donor group. Start the cultivation and solicitation process afresh. It will be easier this time. You've done it. Take a bit of time to review your fundraising plan. What worked well? How could you improve it next time? Review this book. New goals require new planning. Fundraising is a continuous process, one that we hope you find easier as a result of knowing how to design a fundraising plan.

Appendix

The Internet: An Important Tool for Fundraisers

THE INTERNET MAY WELL BECOME one of the most powerful tools a fundraiser has. Ten to fifteen years ago, how many people were using word processors? Can you imagine an office today functioning without one? Within five years the Internet, with its growing ability to provide quick, inexpensive access to potential donors, will take over a huge market share from direct mail. And it will reduce the need to purchase expensive research books and directories that are dated before they arrive at your office. Just as all of us are doing more of our own secretarial duties, we will all be doing a great deal more of our own fundraising research.

The Internet will also reduce the isolation that fundraisers tend to have from their colleagues in other organizations by providing on-line links among fundraisers, so they can gain and give information. For the professional who wants to develop more expertise in an area such as planned giving, membership campaigns, or special events, there will be access to newsgroups, chat rooms, and on-line seminars.

It sounds as though we are touting the Internet as a future fundraisers' cure-all, but just what can it do to help fundraisers today? Here are some of the things other nonprofit professionals are saying about fundraising on the Net.

- "It's like having a library at your fingertips."
- "Our home page is making [our organization] better known."
- "We're offering . . . access to our database of information."
- "E-mail is an ideal way of generating a mailing list."
- "[We can] actually collect contributions over the Internet."

These days almost any computer with a modem can get you to an on-line service that provides easy access to the Internet. A good place to start is with one of the national services, such as America Online ([800] 827–6364) or Prodigy ([800] 776–3449). Take advantage of the free hours these services offer new subscribers to see how the nonprofits mentioned in this chapter are using the Internet.

Although the possibilities may seem endless, you need to determine whether this is the right time for your organization to go on-line. The litmus test is whether the Internet and its user-friendly offspring the World Wide Web can help you complete one or more fundraising tasks cheaper or faster. If you haven't yet "surfed the Web," don't worry; access is easier and cheaper than ever before. You won't be making a big commitment in time and resources by checking out what the Internet has to offer.

Nonprofits are using the Internet for

- Research

- Communication

- Providing services

- Promotion

- Collecting contributions

Research

Giving guidelines, annual reports, and grant lists are available from hundreds of corporations and foundations on the Web. They put this information on electronic pages called Web sites, or home pages. You will find that it is faster and, perhaps, cheaper to browse corporate and foundation giving information on the Web than at your local library. Organizations tailor their Web sites for specific purposes, though, and corporations don't all offer charitable contributions information, so don't give up that library card yet. For example, AT&T has a page with information about the AT&T Foundation at its Web site (www.att.com/foundation), which includes giving statistics, whereas American Airlines (www.americanair.com), for example, gears its Web site exclusively toward serving customers and provides no information on its corporate contributions program.

Here is a short list of corporations and foundations that use their Web sites to provide contributions information.

AT&T Foundation www.att.com/foundation

American Express www.americanexpress.com/corp/
         philanthropy

Ameritech Corporation	www.ameritech.com/news/contributions/index.html
Amoco Foundation	www.amoco.com
Benton Foundation	www.benton.org
Ben & Jerry's Foundation	www.benjerry.com/foundation/index.html
Carnegie Corporation of New York	www.carnegie.org
Digital Equipment Corporation	www.digital.com/info/community/contrib.html
J. Paul Getty Trust	www.getty.edu/grant
GTE Foundation	www.gte.com
John Simon Guggenheim	www.gf.org
Heinz Endowments	www.heinz.org
Hewlett-Packard Company	www.hp.com
IBM Corporation	www.ibm.com/ibm/ibmgives
Japan Foundation	www.jpf.go.jp
Charles A. and Anne Morrow Lindbergh Foundation	www.mtn.org/lindfdtn
George Lucas Educational Foundation	www.Lcf.org
John D. and Catherine T. MacArthur Foundation	www.macfdn.org
Make a Wish Foundation	www.wish.org
Andrew W. Mellon Foundation	www.mellon.org
New York Foundation for the Arts	www.artswire.org
Open Society Institute	www.soros.org
David and Lucille Packard Foundation	www.packfound.org
Pew Charitable Trusts	www.pewtrusts.com

Rockefeller Brothers Fund	www.igc.apc.org/rbf
Rotary Foundation	www.rotary.org
Sega Foundation	www.sega.com
Alfred P. Sloan Foundation	www.sloan.org
Sprint Communications Company	www.sprint.com
Westinghouse Foundation	www.westinghouse.com/corp/ wesfound.htm

Magazines and newspapers, from *U.S. News & World Report* (www.usnews.com) to the *New York Times* (www.nytimes.com), offer free or low-cost searches of past articles. As we discussed earlier, you can learn more about your major gift prospects from articles written about them. Searching individual publication archives on the Internet takes longer than using the Lexis/Nexis (www.lexis-nexis.com) and Dialog (www.dialog.com) information services that charge flat rates, hourly fees, or per article fees. However, the Internet is far less expensive than those services. There is a site on the Internet called the Largest Newspaper Index on the Web! that has links to over three thousand newspapers from more than eighty countries (www.concentric.net/~stevewt). Click on any of the newspapers there, such as the examples in the following list, and you'll be connected to that newspaper's Internet home page.

Albuquerque Journal	www.abqjournal.com
Atlanta Journal	www.ajc.com
Boston Globe	www.boston.com/globe
Chattanooga Times	www.chattimes.com
Chicago Tribune	www.chicago.tribune.com
Dallas Morning News	www.dallasnews.com
Detroit Free Press	www.freep.com
Financial Times (London)	www.ft.com
Hong Kong Standard	www.hkstandard.com

Houston Chronicle	www.chron.com
Izvestia (Moscow)	www.online.ru/mlists/izvestia/izvestia- izvestia
Japan Times	www.japantimes.co.jp
Le Monde (Paris)	www.lemonde.fr
Los Angeles Times	www.latimes.com
Miami Herald	www.herald.com
New York Times	www.nytimes.com
Philadelphia Daily News	www.phillynews.com
Rocky Mountain News	www.denver-rmn.com
St. Petersburg Times (Russia)	www.sptimes.ru
San Francisco Chronicle	www.sfgate.com
Seattle Daily Journal	www.djc.com
Sydney Business Review (Australia)	www.sbr.geko.net.au
Washington Post	www.washingtonpost.com

Communication: E-Mail

Electronic mail offers a fast, reliable means of sending and receiving messages anywhere in the world. You can use it to keep your constituents and donors up to date as well as to communicate with staff and volunteers. It's easier to file and manage e-mail than paper correspondence. You can respond to e-mail messages by writing and sending a personal message or by sending prepared standard replies. A click of the mouse sends your response to the e-mail address or address list of your choice.

Web sites encourage communication. Visitors can simply click on an e-mail address to comment to, respond to, or request information from the Web page sponsor. Believe it or not, it's not difficult to set up a home page. You can even build one in stages. The first things to put on it are your mission statement, your e-mail address, telephone number, and address for regular mail (referred to by *Internauters* as *snail mail*). America Online and Prodigy offer tutorials on how to build a Web page.

E-Mail Pals Can Produce Gems

Web sites aren't like newspaper ads; they're interactive. If you want to know more about an organization, click on its e-mail address (usually at the bottom of the Web page) and send in your questions. A staff member will e-mail a response. If you find an organization with a mission similar to yours, ask where it gets its support and what the staff consider their most effective fundraising tools.

Providing Services

The Internet can help nonprofits deliver services faster and more efficiently. For the National Charities Information Bureau (NCIB) (www.give.org), the charity watchdog agency, the Internet is a godsend. NCIB's mission is to promote informed giving. It accomplishes this by researching and producing reports on nonprofits and by making them available to the public. NCIB's philanthropic standards are on-line, as is its guide to three hundred national charities and other popular reports. Each person who looks at NCIB's Web page is one less phone call that NCIB staff have to field, which usually means one or more fewer brochures to mail. The Internet allows NCIB to reach a wider audience and also helps it save money, time, and resources such as paper, ink, and postage.

These kinds of savings are available to any nonprofit organization that supplies information to its members or constituents. From museum exhibition schedules to school calendars, nonprofits can inexpensively post information on the Net. Have a late-breaking schedule change? No problem. A Web page, like a word-processing document, is instantly upgradable.

Promotion

From highlighting an organization's mission statement to describing its upcoming events and ongoing accomplishments, the Web can act as a giant billboard that gets the word out. In addition, good graphic design can make a Web site's content intriguing and more accessible. Check out the following Web sites, for example, to see how other nonprofit organizations are using the Internet.

American Red Cross	www.redcross.org
Boston Symphony	www.bso.org
Care	www.care.org
Goodwill Industries	www.goodwill.org
Los Angeles Philharmonic	www.laphil.org

Metropolitan Museum of Art	www.metmuseum.org
National Public Radio	www.npr.org
Public Broadcasting Service	www.pbs.org
Salvation Army	www.salvationarmy.org

Even once little-known organizations can become prominent when they have a presence on the World Wide Web. The *Philanthropy Journal of North Carolina* is an example (www.philanthropy-journal.org). Before it got on the Web, not many of its readers were outside North Carolina. Now, in addition to an expanded readership, this regional nonprofit's home page is a well-traveled Web site that maintains one of the most extensive listings of on-line resources for nonprofit organizations.

Collecting Contributions

Your organization can raise money over the Internet. And it's not expensive to set up a digital collection plate. Take a look at the contribution form offered by ReliefNet, a nonprofit organization that encourages support for global relief efforts via the Internet (Exhibit A.1).

Any nonprofit can set up a pledge form on its home page. However, if your nonprofit organization meets ReliefNet's guidelines, you can also start collecting contributions through ReliefNet, as for example the American Friends Service Committee and the American Red Cross do. Organizations participating in ReliefNet must satisfy three requirements:

1. The IRS must recognize the organization as having 501(c)(3) status.

2. The organization must be a member of a federation such as InterAction, which sets standards of accountability, or meet the standards set forth by the National Charities Information Bureau or the Council of Better Business Bureaus's Philanthropic Advisory Service.

3. More than 50 percent of the organization's program expenses must be spent internationally.

Many nonprofits accept credit card donations. The pitfall of doing so on the Internet is that it's not totally secure, and no contributor wants his credit card number intercepted by hackers.

In response to this concern the First Virtual Internet Payment System was developed to provide a simple, secure method for making transactions over the Internet (First Virtual's Web site is www.fv.com). First Virtual stands between consumers and their Internet payments. Before making any Internet transactions, a person who wants to make purchases and contributions over the Net, gives First Virtual his credit card number and receives a First Virtual PIN (personal identification number). The contributor then uses this PIN instead of the credit card number for contributions made over the Internet. First Virtual sends an e-mail message asking the contributor to confirm the request for payment. Only after the contributor replies yes, does First Virtual charge the credit card, through secure financial networks off the Internet. So if a nonprofit accepts First Virtual, donors can make secure Internet contributions that are paid directly into the nonprofit's bank account.

The best way to find out what benefits the Internet might have for your organization is to look at what other nonprofits are doing on the Web. To-Do Exercise A.1 will help you get started.

EXHIBIT A.1

ReliefNet Contribution Form.

ReliefNet™ Contribution Form

- Please fill out the following form.
- **Please note** that the information you provide here will **not** be disclosed and remains the property of the organization to which you have contributed.
- **All** of your contribution goes directly to the organization. ReliefNet keeps **no** portion of your pledge.
- This is a **free** service to relief organizations.
- Before forwarding your pledge, we will reply by email asking for confirmation. We will deliver your pledge less than 24 hours after you confirm it.

First name: _____

Last name: _____

Address 1: _____

Address 2: _____

City: _____

State: ____

Zip/Postal: _____

Country: _____

E-mail address: _____

Source: *ReliefNet Web site: www.reliefnet.org. Reprinted by permission.*

EXHIBIT A.1 (continued)

ReliefNet Contribution Form.

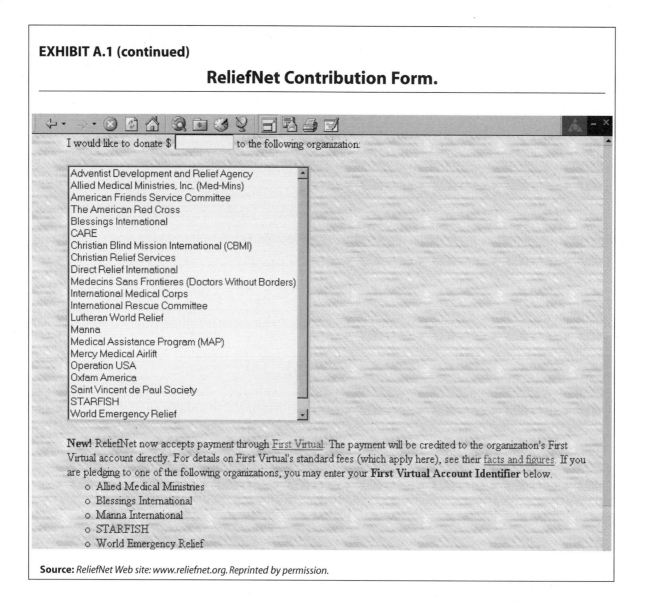

I would like to donate $ [＿＿＿＿＿] to the following organization:

> Adventist Development and Relief Agency
> Allied Medical Ministries, Inc. (Med-Mins)
> American Friends Service Committee
> The American Red Cross
> Blessings International
> CARE
> Christian Blind Mission International (CBMI)
> Christian Relief Services
> Direct Relief International
> Medecins Sans Frontieres (Doctors Without Borders)
> International Medical Corps
> International Rescue Committee
> Lutheran World Relief
> Manna
> Medical Assistance Program (MAP)
> Mercy Medical Airlift
> Operation USA
> Oxfam America
> Saint Vincent de Paul Society
> STARFISH
> World Emergency Relief

New! ReliefNet now accepts payment through First Virtual. The payment will be credited to the organization's First Virtual account directly. For details on First Virtual's standard fees (which apply here), see their facts and figures. If you are pledging to one of the following organizations, you may enter your **First Virtual Account Identifier** below.

- o Allied Medical Ministries
- o Blessings International
- o Manna International
- o STARFISH
- o World Emergency Relief

Source: *ReliefNet Web site: www.reliefnet.org. Reprinted by permission.*

TO-DO EXERCISE A.1

Using the Internet for Fundraising

Although the Web may not yet live up to the hyperbole currently used to describe it, we think you'll find it well worth digging into. Go on-line and check out some of the sites listed in this chapter.

Then use a *search engine* to find the Internet address of a particular corporation or foundation you're interested in. Search engines are software programs that locate Internet home pages. Go on-line and type in one of the following Internet addresses. There are many search engines, but either of the following will do fine.

Webcrawler	webcrawler.com
Yahoo	yahoo.com

These are free services and work like this: a screen pops up with a blank space to type in one or more *keywords* that describe what you're looking for. Type in "Ben & Jerry's Foundation," for example, or any other foundation or corporation you're interested in. Hit return, and a list will appear of sites that have those keywords in their Web page titles. If one of these Web sites interests you, click on it to be connected to it. Browse the site to learn more about the organization.

You may experience some initial frustration as you learn the best kinds of keywords to use and to maneuver around the Web, and be aware that there can be long waits to get to popular Web sites, but there's no substitute for some hands-on exploring. You might want to start with the following four sites. Visiting them will take you on a mini-tour of the nonprofit world on-line. The first two have links to hundreds of nonprofit sites throughout the Web. The other two provide overviews of developments in the nonprofit sector.

The Foundation Center	www.fdncenter.org
Philanthropy Links	www.philanthropy-journal.org
The Council on Foundations	www.cof.org
The Independent Sector	www.indepsec.org

References

Council of Better Business Bureaus, Inc. *Standards for Charitable Solicitations* (pamphlet). Arlington, Va.: Author, 1982.

Foundation Center. *The Foundation Center's User-Friendly Guide: A Grantseeker's Guide to Resources.* (4th ed.) New York: Author, 1994.

Franklin, B. *The Autobiography of Benjamin Franklin* (L. Labaree, ed.). New Haven, Conn.: Yale University Press, 1964.

Hodgkinson, V., and Weitzman, M. S. *Giving and Volunteering 1994.* Washington, D.C.: The Independent Sector, 1994.

Kaplan, A. E. (ed.). *Giving USA 1998.* New York: Trust for Philanthropy, 1998.

McGeady, M. R. "Remarks at Baccalaureate Ceremony—Stanford University." [www.covenanthouse.org]. June 1998.

Rosso, H. A., and Associates. *Achieving Excellence in Fund Raising: A Comprehensive Guide to Principles, Strategies, and Methods.* San Francisco: Jossey-Bass, 1991.

Willett, D. "Missouri Botanical Garden Dedicates State-of-the-Art Research Center." [www.mobot.org/MOBOT/pr/index.html, press release #98032]. March 1998.